EDITORS IN THE STREAM

*Eleven Top Outdoor
Writers On The Purifying Joys
Of Fly Fishing*

EDITED BY TOM TOLNAY

HALO BOOKS
San Francisco

EDITORS IN THE STREAM

Peter Barrett ♦ Dennis Bitton
Silvio Calabi ♦ Jay Cassell ♦ Ed Gray
Nick Lyons ♦ John Randolph
Marty Sherman ♦ Gary Soucie
Vin Sparano ♦ Lamar Underwood

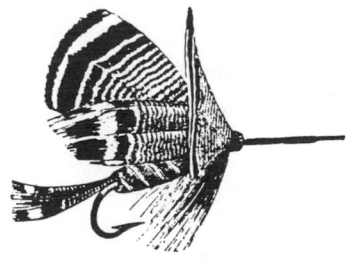

Library of Congress Cataloging-in-Publication Data

Tolnay, Tom, ed.
　　Editors in the Stream: Eleven Top Outdoor Editors on
　　the Purifying Joys of Fly Fishing / edited by Tom
　　Tolnay; with an introduction by Tom Tolnay.

　　p.　cm.

　　ISBN 1-879904-03-9　:　$14.95
　　1. Fly fishing.　I. Tolnay, Thomas.
　　SH456.E29　1992
　　799.1'2—dc20

　　　　　　　　　　　　　　　　　　　　91-34699
　　　　　　　　　　　　　　　　　　　　CIP

© Halo Books, San Francisco, 1992

Halo Books
P.O. Box 2529 ● San Francisco, CA 94126

Cover and interior design by Susan Larson
Typography by BookPrep

CONTENTS

INTRODUCTION

Because of their access to great gear and royal streams, angling editors tend to be thought of more as gurus than as wordsmiths. Yet most editors have to produce a lot of words to get each issue or book out so that the rest of us can sit home and dream a little, leafing through the pages of our favorite outdoor publications—the very ones represented in this new popular edition of *Editors in the Stream: Audubon, Field & Stream, The Flyfisher, Fly Fisherman, Fly Fishing, Fly Rod & Reel, Gray's Sporting Journal, Lyons & Burford, Outdoor Group/ Harris, Outdoor Life, Sports Afield.*

Most often editors find themselves editing or writing copy that explains where to set up your gear, which fly to tie on, and how to cast that fly into a relentless wind. Within these pages, however, these writers take on the mantle of the philosopher, discussing not so much *how* as *why* they fish with flies. For while human instinct and imagination have given rise to countless ways of whiling away the hours and whittling down our troubles which—if you've lived an interesting life—are many, few offer a more profound solace, a more purifying refreshment than standing in a stream with rod and reel in hand, and a pretty tuft of barbed feathers at the end of a virtually invisible tippet.

Between these covers eleven accomplished outdoor editors—Peter Barrett, Dennis Bitton, Silvio Calabi, Jay Cassell, Ed Gray, Nick Lyons, John Randolph, Marty Sherman, Gary Soucie, Vin Sparano, Lamar Underwood—each spin one of their own yarns on the delights and disasters of fly fishing. As professionals in a field which for most of us is recreational, they have a special perspective to share. Sometimes they write dramatically, sometimes humorously, but always convincingly.

They shy away from the idea of being "experts." The reason, perhaps, is that there is so much to learn about this mysterious, downright mystical angling art that they never feel entirely secure in their knowledge! So while the reader may learn a thing or two in the course of turning over the leaves of this handy, handsome edition, the selections were not made on the basis of how so much as why these pros fish with flies.

A word or two of clarification: In these essays, stories and anecdotes the writers did not set out to explain why they wander into a river with a net dangling from their belt, with colorful flies pinned to their chests like medals. It's in the way they tell what happened to them, or what they were thinking about, or were afraid of, that we understand the reasons. And this is true even when their words are not directed at someone in the act of fishing.

Through their far-flung travels and distinct points of view, they let us in on how it feels to fall hopelessly in love with a river, to acknowledge a debt of hard-won skills, to understand relationships through contact with a stream, to be lured by the folklore of this sport, to be caught up in its competitive knot, and especially to know what it's like to be immersed in its environment—wader-deep in cold, rushing, sometimes threatening waters.

With frankness, the editors in the stream discuss their mishaps as well as their successes. For not all these excursions are kindly and tranquil, and sometimes the adversary is not the fish but the elements, or other people . . . or even the self. Yet in each situation there is a clear sense that something memorable is occurring in the life of the angler.

The location of these personal (and group) adventures may shift from the chalk streams of England to the Eskimo rivers of Alaska to Yugoslavia's Sava Bohinjka to the Rogue in Oregon to a tiny, overfished stream in upstate

New York, but the level of committment remains the same—genuinely involved, and the tone remains consistent—a quiet reverence for what a person may see, hear, smell and touch in the right place and time, with the appropriate gear at hand and no more than a creelful of knowledge. To set their hooks into such resplendent possibilities, these editors come armed with an abiding awe for the natural surroundings of fly fishing, and with an eternal respect for the alert species which brims just beneath the surface.

Tom Tolnay, Editor
—*East Branch of the Delaware River, Upstate New York*

Midstream Crisis

By LAMAR UNDERWOOD

S THE YEAR began, I decided to embrace the advice of my friend Sparse Grey Hackle, who told me: "Let the wolf out!" He was dead right. It was the only way to go. No more Mister Nice Guy!

My New Year's resolution was a notice served on all creatures, great and small, that in the open seasons ahead I was going to fill my hand. I was fed up with two-trout days, three-bass weekends and no-deer vacations. I'd had it with calling to bird dogs that wouldn't stand still and turkeys that would [two ridges away!]. I didn't want to see another pheasant getting up 200 yards away down a corn row or another bay full of ducks and geese rafted up and preening their feathers under skies that had flown in from Palm Springs.

Government wags told me that in the previous season some 2.5 million hunters had shot 12 million ducks. The calculator that lives beside my checkbook told me that works out to five or six ducks per hunter. I didn't get any five ducks! Who the hell shot my ducks?

All around, the previous year had not just been bad; it had been a disaster. I zigged when they zagged. The northeasters and I booked into the same places at the same times. I frightened the spots off brown trout while bass slept through my offerings. The deer left the mountain country I hunt, but those from the woods alongside my house found my tulips and peas in the spring, then shredded two young pines during rub-time in the fall. Plenty of geese crossed the pit blinds I hunkered in all season, but they were so high they were a menace to aviation—and they held express tickets.

My dismal performances afield forced me to face what the late John Foster Dulles called "an agonizing reappraisal." Clearly, my tactics were lousy; my timing stank; my equipment belonged in a museum.

I knew better than to seek some all-embracing formula as my game plan. Each subject would have to be tackled separately, tactics and gear made precise. The geese, I felt, would be the simplest

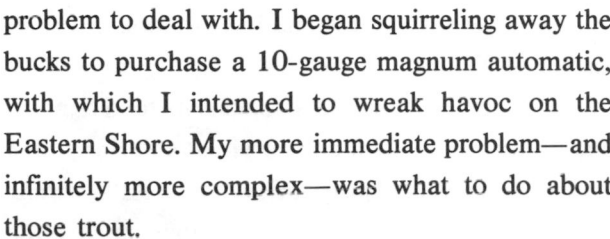

problem to deal with. I began squirreling away the bucks to purchase a 10-gauge magnum automatic, with which I intended to wreak havoc on the Eastern Shore. My more immediate problem—and infinitely more complex—was what to do about those trout.

Since the Romans knew nothing about split-cane rods and matching the hatch, they invented a calendar that starts the new year off from the pit of winter. For me and millions of other fisherman the real new year begins on the opening day of trout season. My usual opening-day scenario looked like this:

An already-pudgy figure, bulked further by enough clothes to outfit the Klondike gold rush, stands hip-deep in a flow of black water torn into sudsy rips by protruding rocks and bearing of the countryside what the winter snows have been holding in storage: sticks, leaves, tires, a bloated cat, the occasional beer can. Overhead the sky is a glowering mass of putty, against which the bare branches of the trees snap and creak with iron-hard stiffness as blasts of wind arrive from Siberia. For hours our man alternates making casts, peering intently at the jaunty little flies that ride the current like miniature galleons, and fumbling stiff fingers through his flybox in search of new offerings. To find a greater fool, you would have to look inside an icefishing shanty.

The bottom of a trout stream is its food factory, and on this day it will not be violated by anything except the soles of el piscator's waders. Although he will soon abandon his dry flies [how quickly the credo fades: "I'd rather catch one on top than five down deep"], our man will make only tentative probes into the depths. His wet flies, streamers and nymphs will sweep harmlessly over the heads of the stone-hugging trout. Troutless by 3 o'clock, he will seek the solace of the ledge where fire, firewater and kindred snake-bit companions will be waiting with tales of woe and livers in various stages of distress.

Long before opening day dawned last season, I was determined to never again be a part of this demented tableau.

For weeks I hit the books with an intensity seldom mounted in my professional life. Schwiebert, Whitlock, Marinaro, Swisher-Richards, Gucci-Nastasi—the great masters of flyfishing for trout were devoured. Their instruction manifested itself in a barrage of catalogs and small packages of flies arriving daily from every corner of troutdom. My wading vest bulged with trinkets. Latin names of bugs came trippingly off the tongue.

Opening day, I stood thigh-deep at the head of a pool of black water, frigid and swollen with runoff. Coming to the stream, I had received the usual assortment of reports that the fish were in a coma. The voice on the car radio had said something about snow. None of these things intimidated me at all. This year I was ready.

To meet this early and elemental trouting condition, I pried open a box of nymphs. These were not ordinary nymphs, but masterpieces of illusion—caterpillar-like, hairy-leggy-juicy-looking. Each was weighted with enough piano wire to outfit a Steinway. Never mind that they would hit the water with the finesse of a slam-dunk. They would go down, my friend, down, down to the very noses of these frozen wisenheimers. I would fish these creations with a leader hacked to three feet. [Long leaders, I had learned, rise in the pushing and swelling of the current]. The whole outfit would ride down with high-density sinking line topped by a fluorescent strike indicator to tell me when I had a customer.

You don't cast such a rig. What you do is sort of heave the whole mess out and to one side, paying close attention that a hook in the ear is not the immediate result of the effort.

I watched the curls of line and leader straighten

downstream toward a boulder that slashed the smooth flow. I tried to form a mental image of what the nymph was doing—sinking, tumbling, ticking over rocks. The line straighteded past the boulder. I paid out three more long pulls from the reel, watching the strike indicator bob on downstream. Suddenly I thought I saw it dart forward. I came back with rod and line and felt the weight of a trout. As the brown—a lovely 15-incher—darted and splashed on the way to the net, my elation soared. My patience and virtue and hard study were to be rewarded. The masters of the game were indeed wise and learned men.

After that, you can imagine my heart-hammering excitement when the next 30 minutes yielded two more fish, about the same size as the first.

Then the devil sent his disciples to descend upon me, like a plague of locusts. First one, then two, then three other anglers were crowding into my stretch of water. Not one asked what I was using. They simply assumed I had found "The Place."

Never mind, I told myself. You can afford to be generous. I waded from the stream and pointed up toward uninhabited water. In a few minutes I was sloshing, much too fast, through a bouldery run of pocket water when I felt my right foot sliding down an eel-slick ledge. I lurched hard to the left, but that leg would not bear the burden. I went down into the water on my back with a teeth-jarring crash. Totally submerged for a second, I stood up and cursed my luck and the worn felt soles of my waders. I was drenched, achingly cold, and clearly out of action for the rest of the day.

As I waded to the edge of the stream, I discovered another result of my accident with dramatic suddeness. As I made a little sideways move with my left leg to step around a rock, I felt a nauseating wave of pain. I did not want to feel such a shock again, ever, so now I picked my way gingerly along, trying to protect the knee.

Yuk! Yuk! See the man all soaking wet and limping toward his car. Fat-ass must've fallen in. Yuk! Yuk!

A prominent physician whom I trust sentenced the knee to six weeks of healing. Because I could not wade the stream, I could not fish for trout. The great fly hatches of early spring for which I had prepared myself so diligently came and went: the Blue Quills, the Hendericksons, the Grannon caddis, the March Browns.

My mood was foul and depressed. Without my jogging program, with which I had successfully been losing weight, I quickly regained ten pounds. Going to work in New York on the train one day I was

struck by a thought as morbid as any I've ever had:
The obituary page of The New York Times named
very few males in their 90s. No, the ages of the boys
getting their names in the paper were in the 70s and
80s. At age 45 I had the startling realization that in
all likelihood I was more than halfway to the barn.
Life begins at 80? Give me a break!

Okay, my somber mood told me, so you've lost
some of your good moves and speed. You can't hit a
60-yard mallard or sink a three-foot putt. On the
tennis court children who can't get into an R-rated
film have you gasping like a beached whale. The
guide can show you a tarpon at 60 feet, and you may
or may not be able to get the fly to it [probably not,
given any kind of wind]. But relax, buster. For the
years have given you wisdom. Look at what you did
with those opening-day trout!

I was still clinging to this slightly uplifting
notion when I finally got back to the river in late
May. One of the year's best hatches remained.
According to the grapevine, the Sulphurs had
arrived in tentative numbers two days earlier, and
all signs pointed to their major emergence late that
evening.

The hatch of *Ephemerella dorothea,* which
goes on with diminishing consistency for about six
weeks on good eastern streams, ranks as a favorite

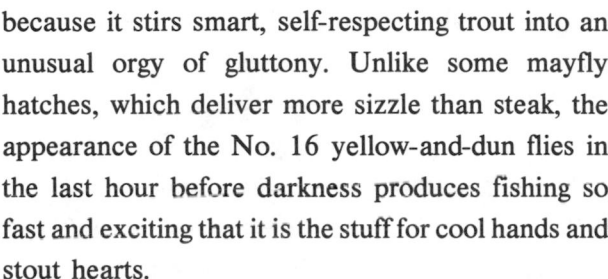

because it stirs smart, self-respecting trout into an unusual orgy of gluttony. Unlike some mayfly hatches, which deliver more sizzle than steak, the appearance of the No. 16 yellow-and-dun flies in the last hour before darkness produces fishing so fast and exciting that it is the stuff for cool hands and stout hearts.

My favorite slick-water was flat empty that evening. My recent misfortune was all forgotten as I waded into position and made a few desultory casts while waiting for the hatch to begin. The air was heavy with humidity, and low clouds on the ridges promised that darkness would come early and perhaps a thunderstorm with it.

The time that passed seemed interminable. Nothing came off the darkening water, not even caddis. A kingfisher flew upstream, scolding my presence. I heard a great horned owl up on the mountain and an answering cry from nearby. Then I saw the first delicate yellow mayfly climbing steeply toward the trees. In a few moments there was another, then another, then another, and then I actually saw one in the instant it left the water—and beyond it the swirl of a trout.

My line arched through the growing dusk. I saw my artificial Sulphur begin its jaunty ride down the feeding lane where the trout had swirled. It floated on downstream unharmed. There were other rises all over the pool now—not splashy water-throwing slaps, but subtle bulges and swirls.

I really started worrying when my bogus Sulphur made three more rides through the melee without interesting a trout. What was wrong? The fly? The leader? My thoughts screamed as I watched the hatch and rises go on: You've been out of action so long you don't know what you're doing.

In the middle of this burst of self-condemnation I saw something—flashes of darting trout just beneath the surface. That was it! The trout were not taking the surface duns! They were nymphing, gulping the insects as they rose to the surface and in the film as they emerged into winged shape.

I was prepared for this, but my hands trembled as I opened the flybox and got out a floating nymph. The light was going fast, but I managed to tie on the fly without digging out my night light. In my excitement, however, I dropped my reading half-glasses into the stream. Klutz! Fool! I should have had them on a cord around my neck.

No matter. I had the right ammo now, and the fish were still going strong as I roll-cast the nymph to the top of the pool. Instantly a trout was on, and I felt a flush of ultimate satisfaction.

The fish was a strong pulsating weight as it struggled upstream for a few seconds. Then the line went slack as the trout bolted down-stream almost past my legs, a momentary shadow that caused me to gasp: I was into my largest trout ever.

The reel screamed appropriately as the fish bolted downstream. He reached the lip of the falls that terminated the pool and turned to face the current. The steady pressure on the 5X felt unbelievable. I had the feeling of the fish backing up, backing to the edge of the tumbling water. He was going to be washed over the lip! I had to do something! I palmed the flange of the reel, increasing the drag, and thereby succeeded in instantly breaking off the trout as surely as though I'd been trying to.

I reeled in the sickeningly slack line and looked at the 5X tippet. So many trout were still taking the sulphur nymphs all over the pool that the excitement smothered the loss of the big fish. I quickly had another floating nymph out, ready to tie on. I felt my shirt pocket for my reading glasses and remembered where they had gone. I held the fly at arm's length against the gloom of the darkening sky. No way. I could not thread the eye of the hook in that dimness.

No problem. My night light had a magnifying

glass that fit over the top of the light. No sweat, just stay cool.

I was deeply aware of the rises continuing all over the pool as I pulled the light out and draped its cord around my neck. I felt deeper into the pocket for the magnifying glass. It wasn't there! I flipped the switch on the light. Nothing! *Click, click. Click, click.* Still nothing! Okay, the batteries are dead. You're on your own. Now just hold the fly very still against what is left of the sky and tie it on.

My panic rose as I tried unsuccessfully to tie on the No. 16 Sulphur. I tried a No. 14. It would not go. In a final burst of madness and inspiration, I dug out a No. 10 Blonde Wulff, the biggest fly in my vest. Maybe it would work on these feeding fish.

Perhaps it would have. I don't know. I never got the Wulff tied on. My vision is 20-20, but at age 45 I could not see close up well enough to tie on a fly and resume fishing a hatch that I had waited for all winter.

I reeled in slowly, felt the end of the leader reach the reel, then broke down my rod. The splashes of feeding trout popped out from the darkness. I could not see the rises now, but they were distinctive above the murmur the current made as it tailed from the pool downstream.

Slowly the disappointment drained away. The

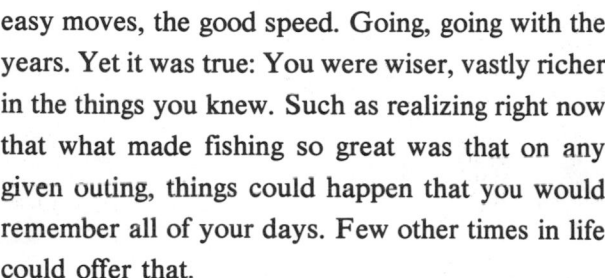

easy moves, the good speed. Going, going with the years. Yet it was true: You were wiser, vastly richer in the things you knew. Such as realizing right now that what made fishing so great was that on any given outing, things could happen that you would remember all of your days. Few other times in life could offer that.

That is the easy part of change—the knowing, the feeling. The other side is that you have left something precious behind—something you had used up and would have to go on without.

Flashes of lightning came across the ridgetop, then the roll of advancing thunder. The feeding grew quieter, then died out completely. The bursts of lightning helped me find my way up the hillside to the lane that led back to the car.

I did not know if I had reached the end of something or the beginning.

The wind blew on the high ridges, gusting along the slopes, coming down to the river.

River Of Dreams

By **SILVIO CALABI**

N THE VERY FIRST NIGHT in camp I encountered the two biggest fish I've ever seen in fresh water. Now, months later, it has the surreal quality of a dream.

Primed for a week in the Alaskan bush, brimming with the enthusiasm of new arrivals, we three sports had plunged into Birch Creek straight-away after supper and fairly jitter-bugged through the pools near camp: We were *here,* this is *it!* *Alaska,* man! Sheer adrenaline can work miracles, but like the northern twilight, it eventually seeps away. By midnight, jet lag had surpassed all other considerations, and I was letting the current guide my steps back downstream to the tents.

In a bumpy section no wider than a moderate cast and hemmed in by rock walls, I met the fish, a mating pair of king salmon. I entered the rapid from above; the two red torpedoes swam up from below. Even in the subartic dusk, I could see their wakes. As the water shallowed, their dorsals and then their backs and tails broke the surface. They pushed up over the first gravel bar, dropped into a narrow channel of deeper water, and then spotted me watching them. The spawning urge must have been on them; there stood a bear-sized creature in the stream, yet they shot towards me, then yeered off for an end-run.

My first impulse, I admit, was to let them by. There wasn't much room, and the smaller one looked to be 50 pounds. His girl-friend was the scary one—if he was 50, she had to go 75 or better. Two years before, farther south along the Bering coast, a mere 17-pound king had crashed into me while trying to escape a hook, and had nearly tipped me sunny-side down. This pair looked like they could break legs. But I gathered my courage— *They're just aiming to get by, not attacking*—and ran to block them off. They feinted; I followed. They hung back to wait. I felt almost as trapped, in the top of the run; we were in checkmate.

The weariness was gone. I was as charged up

as I've been, fishing. I shook out line and began to work a streamer past their noses. It seemed unlikely they would strike in such a situation, but maybe one was just aggressive enough to overcome its fears. And I'd never know unless I tried. In the gloom, and with a genuine case of buck fever, I had considerable difficulty in getting a decent presentation. When I did, the two salmon simply ignored the fly; it twitched off past them and then, to my annoyance, was hit hard by a rainbow tagging along to wait for salmon spawn. Only in Alaska can an angler be frustrated, disgusted and peeved by the inadvertent strike of a four-pound trout. And only in Alaska can he sight-fish to such champions as this pair of amorous battlewagons.

The salmon had enough and retreated back down into deeper, wider water. The red shapes were there one minute, gone the next. I gathered up my line and waddled on home, by now almost staggering on my feet. I couldn't have endured an hour or two of frantic fish-fighting then anyway.

"Birch Creek" doesn't appear on any Alaska maps. It's a name that the camp owners [Ron and Maggie McMillan and Rick and Patty Grant, of Bristol Bay Lodge fame] coined to try to divert attention—and thus angling pressure—away from the river. I'm not going to spill the beans either, but now I'm going to make a statement that can't be made more than once or twice in a lifetime: My stay at Birch was the best week of fishing I've ever had.

From a Beaver a thousand feet up and three miles away, the camp appears inconsequential—two brown and two green spots on a greener hillside next to a silver-blue river. In midsummer the planes have to land on a tundra pond on the far side of the hill, and guides and cook meet you there, to help in humping supplies and gear over the path to camp.

While the "mother lodge," back on Lake Aleknagik, boasts picture windows, an acre of decks, sauna and a hot tub big enough to have its own spawning run, Birch Creek Camp gets by with a pair of large quonset-type tents—one for the cooking and dining, the other for guests—set on plywood floors. The style is the same; the differences are of degree. In camp, the fisherman's Alaska is right there, just outside the tent flap. There's no need to climb into a boat or a plane. The fish are—right there. With a maximum of four guests in camp, the morning prep time can be reduced considerably. Two fishermen and a guide per boat means that an hour after getting up you can

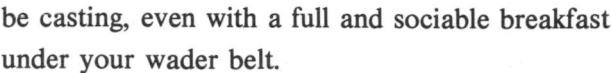

be casting, even with a full and sociable breakfast under your wader belt.

[To avoid overfishing, the guides motor up- or downriver every day to different "beats," which are then covered on foot. In a week, you never fish the same water twice. Nor is there any need to; here at least, the quality of the fishing seems consistently high throughout.]

Evenings, while supper waits, you sit on the cooktent stoop and count salmon [species and individuals] parading through the long, still pool below. Even in thigh-deep water, the big kings leave wakes behind as they bulldoze on upstream. Others jump, for no apparent reason, sometimes three or four times in succession.

It's mid-July and so the dog salmon are already beginning to die. With their vertical, irregular red-on-green mottling they can be recognized as readily as the pink kings. The sockeyes are bigger than the dogs, smaller than the kings, also going to red, but with dark-green heads. And the pink salmon, the little humpbacks, are still fish-colored now. You can't see them from the stoop unless the light is just right. If you stir yourself and go sit on the riverbank, then you can see humpies and cruising trout, occasional grayling and the metallic flash of Dolly Varden. These waters hold seven kinds of gamefish at once. Later in the summer, silver salmon, the coho, swim up from the ocean.

When the salmon move into fresh water in great numbers, they tend to put the trout down for a few weeks. We were lucky; although the sun-run species were in, the trout were still actively taking our flies, both wet and dry. There was little insect activity, yet bushy dries drew plenty of attention; the most effective surface pattern was not an insect imitation at all, but a mouse—preferably large, scraggly, waterlogged and tied with caribou hair.

We fished them western-style, banging the banks hard. Flop the mouse onto the water, then skitter it away from shore, using rod tip and current to make a surging wake. The big rainbows bolted from their lies to give chase, sometimes missing again and again before connecting with a violent strike. One hit five times on the same retrieve; another, obviously ticked off, slapped the mouse with its tail and sent it spinning into the air before diving onto it. If a fish missed every time, it was a simple matter to rest it a few minutes, then go back for another series of wild charges. On the first day, we killed a trout that had been hooked deeply on a Woolly Bugger. In his stomach were three tremendous tundra mice, or lemmings. The Dolly

Varden we took every day for shore lunch had almost all been eating mice as well.

The rainbows were all alike as cookies from the same tin. Most were 20 to 24 inches long, with vivid red streaks extended from flanks up onto gills and cheeks, and vibrant black spots on tails and bodies. They had the proportions and air of wild things that are well fed and ecologically secure; shrinking violets don't make the cut in Alaska. If our flies were mice, it was easy to think of the trout as cats—aggressive, graceful, sometimes almost playful. But predators above all, accomplished and deadly. They liked the caribou hair and would chew the fly and hold it and tug for long seconds after we tried to move it in their mouths to drive home the hook.

The trout—along with everything else— took wet flies, too. The fish seemed poised between early season, when they usually hit anything black or brown or dark olive [fished low and slow], and high summer, when their preferences shift to red [as in salmon spawn]. Muddlers, Matukas, Woolly Buggers, big Girdle Bugs all drew strikes, as did Pink Ladies, Aztecs, Babines and other crazy bright patterns. Since there was no call for long leaders, we fished shooting heads and sinking lines even in shallow, relatively quiet water.

When the mousing slowed down, or we wanted bigger fish, we switched to wet gear.

The dogs—chum salmon—were beginning to die. They were there in the greatest numbers, and while every day we took individuals that were still vigorous, every morning we discovered fresh carcasses washed ashore on the gravel bars. Then the swifter deterioration began; the eyes went first, to gulls and ravens. If a larger animal didn't drag the whole thing away, then insects began tunneling in and in a few days all that remained were skin and skeleton, like a deflated salmon balloon.

By the end of the week, the dogs were dying more noticeably, around our feet, while we watched. Ancient-looking fish would appear, grey and greasy yellow, bony-jawed, literally in tatters, spawned out but still struggling to answer the call to swim upstream. Anal fins and lower tail were invariably gone, wasted by the fish's inability to eat and then scraped away by a hundred passages over rocks and riffles. Each salmon eventually reached a chute somewhere in the river where the current was too much. The fish would die there, repeatedly and ever more slowly swimming up and being repulsed until it turned turtle and drifted away, finally headed downstream.

While the pools around us bloomed with the V-wakes of living, hungry, feeding and spawning fish, the down side of the cycle was there too. Life into death, death into life—couplings in a food chain older than the river itself.

Shore lunches here are almost luxurious, and they can more than replace the calories burned off by cold water and wind. Although the countryside is tundra, the waterway and its sediments support small trees, and the hills break enough of the wind to let them grow. Consequently there's firewood—deadfalls and driftwood bleached by the sun. The guides beach their skiffs while we fish on, and soon they're working over a cooking-bed of red coals. The entree remains the same—fillet of Dolly Varden, sauteed and served with skillet-fried onions and potatoes. As appetizer, perhaps a mug of chicken soup, a by-product of last night's supper; for side dishes, rolls and butter, canned corn or green beans. And for dessert, toll house cookies [big ones, baked the evening before, with lots of chocolate chips and brown sugar to make them chewy], pastry, carrot cake. There's cowboy coffee and cans of soda and even beer. My waders seemed to shrink daily.

In the evenings, it's even better and more relaxed. The excitement of the day supports you just long enough to stow the gear and get into camp clothes. While supper cooks, there's time to watch the river over the rim of a glass. [Yes, there's ice in the gas-fired refrigerator-freezer.] At northern latitudes, evenings last for hours. Coffee, dessert, diary-keeping, tackle-mending, fly-tying, conversation, a game of Trivial Pursuit [never challenge a journalist-editor who grew up in the 60's] and even more fishing, for those whose day went by too quickly. With bed and board 40 feet from the river's edge, post-prandial angling is a matter of a minute's walk and hardly requires the attendance of a guide. It's safe—although we see fresh sign daily, bears shy away from camp and the noise of the outboards in the morning clears them out of the river.

Midweek, we traveled downstream several miles to where the river forks out and braids into channels, and fished roaring little sluices and still, deep holes and brushy cutbacks. Regularly, a trout came charging out from the overhangs, its open mouth showing white in the green water, to slaughter a mouse. The day began dark, clammy and cold, but by mid-morning the fog had burned away and the sun shone on us. The fishing improved as the sun climbed.

Eventually we arrived at a long, straight pool with a beach on one shore and a high bank on the other. There were ghostly reddish shapes hovering in the depths of the center channel. Other salmon passed by in the shallower water and behind them swam grayling and Dollies and rainbows, waiting for spawning to begin. It was early for the kings to spawn, and we could see none of the sofa-sized redds they build. I waded in at the upstream end and began to drift a Babine, low and slow, through the herd. A big hit—too enthusiastic to be a big salmon, too red to be a trout. It was a jack, an immature king, of about five pounds. A few more casts and then there was a great commotion out in the middle of the pool and a very solid strike. This was 20 pounds of king salmon, a handsome, red-bronze creature that tore up and down for 20 minutes before consenting to be handled, photographed and released. It was the first good fly-caught king.

The others went farther downstream. Andy, one of the guides, stayed with me while I worked the pool some more. In an hour, I took a couple of trout and hit and immediately lost two of the big salmon. Their takes were almost imperceptible—fly and line simply stopped in the water. I reared back hard, preferring to lose a fish at the outset instead of after an hour's labor. Both fish came right away to the surface, thrashed and were gone. I had to sit and recover after each one.

Then we went into a dry spell. Andy and I worked up and down the hole for half an hour. Finally we went back for a last try in a narrow slot where dozens of kings had passed through while we ate, sometimes churning the water like outboard motors. From a cast away upstream, I could see new fish there. I quartered the fly across current, let it sink, and monitored its progress into the top of the slot. Lost sight of the fly. There was a solid pull and I was fast to a huge salmon. His head broke out of the water and then a tail like a shovel came up and splashed water into the trees. Andy and I screamed; the fish took off downstream; and Andy ran to push the boat off and follow.

Even with waders down around my waist, I could cross and recross the river. Although the salmon took about 150 yards of line right away, I had plenty left and it was unlikely this big ocean fish would intentionally tangle me in the brush along the cutbank. The leader was short and stout. The various connections had been tested and proven. Again preferring to lose the fish sooner than later, I put everything I could against him, tried to snub him while reeling myself downstream, but in reality I reeled and ran.

It was half a mile of river before we caught up with the fish and the others. Birch Creek flowed out of the woods into another, longer pool, again with a broad beach on one side. The salmon had breached five times now—elephantine thrashings that turned my knees to jelly and made me shout. At the top of the new pool, I threw him some slack and ran down the beach. Without the goad of the line, he made his only mistake: He stopped running for the sea, and let me get below him. Now I could hold him into the current, make him fight me and the river. When he turned downstream, I chased him through the crotch-deep water to cut him off.

When he sulked, immovable, on the sandy bottom, I slapped the bowed rod on the water and shuffled towards him until he broke and ran away. He was beaten if I could hold on.

I rehearsed what I would do and say when the hook pulled free. Alternately, I decided I'd be cool and philosophical or furious and determined to try again. Miraculously, it wasn't necessary: After an hour and a half, the salmon swung around me into a down-stream arc and let himself be beached. Both guides fell on him. The others cocked their cameras. I stared and let my arms stretch out their length.

We had no scale large enough to weigh such a fish. He was four feet long, probably 50 to 55 pounds. I knelt in the shallows with him cradled and coddled him. Talked to him. I wanted him to go back and breed lots of new salmon who would also look favorably upon fishermen's flies. He was happy to oblige.

For the rest of the week, I sported a saucer-sized bruise under my sternum. When home again, I sent the rod back to have the reel seat drilled out for a fighting butt.

Saturday, always the last day in a fishing camp, came up foggy and cold and still, but by 10 it was again blue and warm. Sarah, the chef, joined us again and the whole party slowly moved upstream, looking for new fish and experiences to end the week with. We were relaxed and jovial, appreciative of everything—the crystalline water and sandy bottom, last scraps of fog turned to silver by the sun, the line of a rocky scarp against the deep blue sky. We all knew it had been an unusual time.

By early afternoon we'd floated back to camp. Gear was strewn everywhere; waders draped over the tents to dry, rod tubes came out from under bunks, flies plucked from hats and vests returned to their boxes. The three who were leaving appeared, one by one, in travel clothes outlandish and formal after a week in sweat pants and wool shirts. An airplane materialized, with four strangers on board, and so began the journey back into the rat race.

Minor Tactics On An English Chalkstream

By **NICK LYONS**

N ENGLISH CHALKSTREAM is a gentle, pastoral part of this frantic world. Limpid green and translucent, the river glides clear and steadily over flowing waterweed. Here and there a swallow or marten or finch dips and glides. Herefords graze in the lush meadow. Protected for centuries, guarded by riverkeeper and rule and club fiat, the water and its world are much like they were a thousand years ago. Yet on such gentle waters, within the frame of carefully fashioned codes, mighty dramas often transpire.

From a busy week in London, an American went one morning to the "Wilderness" section of the River Kennet in Berkshire, one of the noblest of the chalkstreams. The Kennet, carefully tended by the good riverkeeper Bernard, grows lusty trout to test the highest art of skilled fly fishers. John Goddard, who has taken three- and four-pound brown trout from these storied waters, usually passes the stern test. The American could not have had a better guide. And he had the company of Timothy Benn to advise him wisely about tactics.

The American had been to this river before. He had fished the Kennet several years earlier, for twelve hours. There were good trout in the Kennet—two- and three-pound browns—and he had seen many of them that day. You had to be careful to see the fish before the fish saw you, and the fish should be "on the fin," feeding. That was the code. You fished to the fish; you did not fish the water. And you fished only upstream, with a floating line. Often you had to kneel so that the trout would not see you, and the American marveled later that he had spent most of that day in the praying position, although, perhaps mistakenly, not for spiritual guidance. Often the casts had to be guided with deft skill through the maze of low branches, back branches and high border weeds; the American only sometimes managed this but felt his flies lent a festive touch to the trees. And the trout spooked easily. The American had not gotten one of those large Kennet browns to move toward one of his flies.

But for two years he had dreamed of the river and his dreams were mingled with the most cunning scheming. This time he was not without strategies. He had studied the minor tactics. He had learned the puddle cast. And he carried his lucky net.

Then, that morning, working hard and fishing to two or three good trout on the fin, he'd moved precisely no fish. He was not up to it. It was my youth, he thought in a paroxysm of shame, misspent worming and spinning. I am unworthy. And there is too little time to train the eye and hand for such noble work, let alone cleanse the soul.

The three had a pleasant lunch near the river, drank some wine, ate pate, laughed, told tales, and then headed out again. Neil Patterson, a young friend who lived on the river and would meet them later, had left a map for the American indicating that in the upper region there were some "very interesting trout."

The wine had been cool and pleasant and the American had perhaps drunk a glass too much of it, which made three. He did not count as one of his very few virtues the ability to drink much wine or to remember the names of the wines he had drunk. They all sounded French. The afternoon was warm and he had eaten well and he had had that extra glass of wine, and he was feeling very content and hopeful when John Goddard spotted a steadily rising fish of about two pounds at the head of a broad pool. This proved to be a most interesting trout. Despite two slap casts, three linings and an hour of more delicate work, the fish was still rising merrily to naturals with very slow, very deliberate rises. He is lunching at Simpson's, the American thought, and he has paid a pretty ten pounds sterling for the privilege and he will not be disturbed by the traffic on the Strand or the punk-rock crowds at the Lyceum. He is quite intent on the business at hand and knows precisely what he has ordered.

So the American was pleased when John Goddard called downstream, "When you've had enough of him, come up here. I've spotted an interesting fish." Timothy Benn, who had taken a fine two-pounder that morning, positioned himself upstream with a camera to record properly the confrontation of the American with this new interesting trout.

The fish was feeding in a one-foot eddy behind a knobby root on the opposite side of the river. The

American knew that the fish would not move an inch from that spot any more than the Simpson's trout would be disturbed at his selective lunching. He knew that an exceptional cast was needed—upstream, with some particular loops of slack, in close to the bank—for the fly to catch the feeding lane and float into the trout's dining room without drag. A puddle cast.

After four short casts and another two that led to drag, the American was sure he could not manage this minor tactic. It was subtler fishing than he was used to, and he was not impressed with his ability to move Kennet trout. But he had not put it down. The occasional sip-rises in the eddy continued. The fish might be quite large.

And then the American managed an able puddle cast beyond his wildest hopes and the fly floated a foot or two and went calmly into the trout's domain, and he heard someone whisper, "He'll come this time," and, miracle of miracles, the trout did.

The trout rose, was hooked, made a low jump, came clear of the stump and then streaked downstream, its back bulging the surface, its force bending the bamboo rod sharply. A very good fish. Better than two pounds.

From that point on, the American was not sure

why he acted the way he did. Perhaps it was that he had just read something about getting below a fish, which proved that fishermen should read fewer books. Perhaps it was the extra glass of wine. More likely it was pure panic.

The American bolted. He began high-stepping downriver, busting, bursting the pastoral quiet of the chalkstream with his wild splashes. He heard one of his companions, in a high, incredulous, voice ask: "*Where* are you going?"

The trout, which had never witnessed a performance like this, and considered it extremely poor form, raced farther from the area in sheer embarrassment.

Then the American did something else he later could not explain. With the trout still green, he grasped for his lucky net.

The net was of the teardrop variety and had been bought in the Catskills and treasured for many years. The American carried it loose in his ArctiCreel, where it was safe from the brush. In fact, only a half hour earlier he had advised his English friends that this was a much more suitable net than the long-handled nets they carried, and that it could be carried in the creel, safe from brush, out of harm's way, until needed.

The American grasped the handle of the net

and wrestled it from his creel. In so doing, out came his fly box. This was his prized fly box, a Wheatley, the most expensive kind of Wheatley, with compartments on both sides, and he had filled it for this trip with some of his choicest flies— flies by Flick and Troth and Whitlock and Leiser.

The fly box twisted in the meshes of the tangled net bag, teetered on the rim while the American did a jib and a hop, midstream, then popped free and landed open on the limpid waters of the Kennet and began to float serenely off to the left.

The trout was headed right.

The gentlemen with the camera was reloading film at the precise moment the American had to choose between the fly box or the trout, so there is no visual record of the sudden swerve to the left, the deft netting of one fat Wheatley fly box; and since the trout had turned the bend, no one except the American saw the roll on the surface and the positive smirk as one very interesting trout rejoiced that on the other end of the line there had been such a raving maniac.

Later, the men gathered near the bridge on the main river and drank a bit more wine. Neil Patterson and another pleasant member of the club were with them now and there was good talk and the spirited camaraderie uniquely possible along trout streams. Someone suggested that the Simpson's trout was merely one of Patterson's tethered pets, and someone else suggested that it was good the American's fly had pulled loose from the interesting trout because Bernard did not like his Kennet browns festooned like Christmas trees. The American was quietly satisfied that he would never have stooped quite so low as that.

Then John Goddard mentioned the big trout beneath the bridge and the American was invited to have a go at him. Not for me, he thought. Old Oscar—the not-to-be-caught behemoth brown. Not that fish—and not with this audience.

But the fish was high in the water, on the fin, taking the odd sedge a few feet under the bridge, and in a few moments, unable to resist, the American was tying on a Colorado King with shaky hands, squinting into the angular sun. And a few moments later he had made a truly classic puddle cast, holding the rod high and stopping the line short so that the current had three feet of slack to consume before the fly dragged.

The fly came down three inches from Old Oscar's nose. The chorus of onlookers, standing in a semi-circle behind him, grew ominously silent. Old

Oscar turned and floated down with the fly a few inches. The chorus audibly released breath, in a quiet whoosh.

Old Oscar took.

And the American struck, with no time to think of all the subtle minor tactics he had learned . . . and neatly snapped the fly off in the fish.

The Night Jump

By **GARY SOUCIE**

T WAS OUR LAST fishing day in Yugoslavia, and our fishing guides proposed that we do a "night jump." I don't know what it's called in Slovene, but our English-speaking tour guide said that's how it translated. Our fishing guides for the Sava Bohinjka, Joze Borisek and Vojko [Vojc] Carl, riverkeepers and wardens for *Zavod za Ribistvo Slovenija* [the Fishing Research Institute of Slovenia], spoke little English and therefore couldn't help much. When you fish strange waters in strange lands, something always seems to get lost in translation.

As nearly as we could figure it out, a night jump is fast-moving wade fishing at day's end, when fish typically "turn on" and start feeding. It seemed a pretty good plan to us, and the women probably would have followed Vojc anywhere. So we hopped into the van and headed downriver from the Hotel Zlatorog on the western end of Lake Bohinj until we reached a spot a few kilometers below the town of Bohinjska Bistrica. There we split into two parties.

Vojc, Ed Ricciuti, Martha Hill, and I would wade downstream. Joze, Dave Finkelstein, Jack London, and Evelyn Letfuss would travel a few kilometers ahead in the van and wade upstream toward us. The plan was to rendezvous at a bridge midway between our starting points, then move [jump?] to another spot before it got dark. We were warned not to dawdle; we were to reach that bridge by seven o'clock. This would be to most wade fishing what running is to jogging.

The night jump got off to an inauspicious start. Even before we had divided up and set off on our separate ways, Jack realized that he had left his wading boots in Ljubljana, where he and Ed had spent an extra day doing research. After spending a few minutes contemplating his now-useless stockingfoot waders in a silent Irish rage, Jack decided he would fish by walking alongside the river. [He would spend this first half of his night jump struggling through bankside willow thickets and walking around streamside houseyards.] Ed, who hadn't yet fished the Sava Bohinjka, had decided to bring along the bottom half of a two-piece wet suit rather than waders, and neoprene diving booties rather than wading boots. [He would discover how different this river was from the others we had fished, and would spend his night jump ouch-ouching over the rocky sections and wading into trouble in the deep holes.] Dave, an aging karate nut who was still recovering from major hip surgery, was wondering how he would fare, wading so fast and far—having already spent a morning and an afternoon slogging through some of the coldest, fastest, trickiest, prettiest water any of us had ever seen. [He would get wet.] At least the women and the guides were ready.

Me? I had my equipment problems, too. To save weight and bulk on the trip, I had decided to leave my wading boots at home and use instead a large pair of basketball shoes to which I had glued felt wading soles. The felt soles had come off on the first day of fishing, about ten days earlier on the Gacka River in Croatia. I am willing to testify under solemn oath that rubber-soled basketball shoes are not the footwear of choice for fast alpine rivers flowing over marble and limestone rocks, pebbles, and gravel. I had also discovered—via bruised and swollen ankles—why wading shoes are made of heavy, sturdy leather instead of light, flimsy canvas.

Before getting started on our night jump, let me tell you a little about this river we were fishing.

After rising from a spring in Tryflav National Park, high in the Julian Alps on the shoulder of a mountain called Kanjavec, the Sava Bohinjka almost immediately makes a dramatic plunge down the falls called Slap Savica. It then flows under the shadow of the ski lifts and runs of Vogel, and into Lake Bohinj, which supports a population of alpine char as well as Europe's—and possibly the world's—largest grayling hatchery. [This world-class hatchery is an incredibly primitive-looking operation with little more than some pipes bearing mountain spring water to a row of circular concrete tanks, a lake boat that pulls a plankton net to catch food for the grayling fry, and a German shepherd on a clothesline for security. No buildings, no laboratories, no machinery. And it works. The tanks were full of inch-long fry when we had visited it the previous afternoon, and the day after our departure Joze and Vojc would be preparing 50,000 fry for shipment to Austria and another half million to Germany.]

Try to imagine a swift mountain stream whose clarity and blue-green waters rival those of the Caribbean: That's the Sava Bohinjka in its uppermost reaches, where it never exceeds five or ten meters in width. You can see the dark shadows of fish in every pool and you know they are hiding there under the silvery, impenetrable surfaces of every run and riffle. But fishing isn't allowed up here because of the back-cast dangers to tourists hiking up to the falls and milling about the footbridge behind the chalet-like Hotel Zlatorog. Downstream from the footbridge, though, the hiking paths angle away from the stream, out of its tiny flood plain, and the fishing waters begin. Here, just before it spills into Lake Bohinj, the river widens, broadens, slows a bit, and picks up the milklike cloudiness we tend to associate with chalkstreams.

Where it flows out of the eastern end of the lake, under a quaint stone bridge and past an impossibly picturesque little church, the Sava Bohinjka is more typically the color of mountain streams, where you can see any color at all between the foamy white and glittering silver of the rapids. Dave, Evelyn, Marty, and I had fished this section the previous morning, while Jack and Ed were on their way up from Ljubljana, and we had been baffled by it.

It was the fastest water I had ever fished. Several big trout were holding in an eddy pool on the other side, where a brook entered the Sava Bohinjka. You could reach the pool with a cast, but the raging current would sweep the line away even before the fly had settled. [It was, of course, illegal to fish from the opposite bank, where the trees would have prevented casting in any event.] I tried wading out into the rapids just above the inflow and holding pool, and came closer to drowning than to presenting a fly in that pool. As for fishing the run below the rapids, there were lots of fly-eating trees hanging low over the channel on the opposite side, and I just couldn't seem to get the hang of fishing five-second drifts at ten or fifteen knots.

It also didn't help that we had attracted a throng of onlookers, who kept pointing at us and chattering in Slovene. They might have been trying to be helpful, but we couldn't understand them, and their attention just made us self-conscious and all the more inept. [There had been a fishing tournament here immediately preceding our visit, and the more I struggled the more I became convinced that these were Slovenia's, if not all of Yugo-elite, who had lingered specifically for the purpose of witnessing our humiliation and angling self-immolation.] We managed to catch a few fish in spite of our skills.

Farther downstream the Sava Bohinjka runs alternately clear, dark, chalky, and myriad variations on blue-green, depending upon the bottom, the depth, the nature of the tributary rivulets, and the color temperature of the sky. No matter its color, and in every manifestation, it is a beautiful river. And it is full of fish: brown trout, rainbows, grayling. After it joins the Sava Dolinka a few kilometers southeast of the alpine resort town of Bled, near Radovljic, it becomes the big, dark, stately Sava River and flows to join the Danube at Belgrade. At 940 kilometers [584 miles], it is Yugoslavia's longest river and the second longest of the Danube's three hundred tributaries. In the Sava proper, the trout and grayling begin to give way to pike, asp, carp, barbel, wels, and all sorts of cyprinids and other warm-water fish that are the eagerly sought prey of the so-called "coarse" fishermen, who far outnumber fly fisherman.

Back to the night jump.

Even before the van rumbled off bearing the rest of our party downstream, Vojc waded into the river and started casting. I followed close behind, trying to learn through hand signals and facial gestures whether there were any deep holes that had to be avoided, where to begin fishing, and how to proceed. Wading downstream and fishing dry flies upstream may be a piece of cake for truly competent fly fishermen, but I'm not and it wasn't. I tried imitating Vojc but my casting was too slow and my wading too precarious to get the rhythm of his cast-cast-cast-curse-slip-curse-teeter-curse-pivot-totter-curse-cast-cast-cast-curse. My night jump was off to a very slow start, more nearly resembling a twilight crawl.

By the time I had fished one riffle and the head of a pool, Vojc was nearly out of sight around a bend downstream. Marty was having the same trouble I was, and opted for casting from shore. Ed discovered that scuba booties designed for walking on sandy bottoms and even big reefs are no match for broken marble and limestone bottoms, so he scampered along the edge of the river toward the sandy-banked section downstream, looking like a man walking on eggshells, very sharp eggshells. As it turned out, it was lucky for Ed that he had rushed ahead to catch up with Vojc; two or three times, Ed waded too deeply into a pool to get back out under his own steam. For the time being, Marty and I had this little section of the river to ourselves. She had discovered a little mill outlet on her side of the river where several trout were holding close to shore in a spot where the current had undercut some limestone slabs. Because of the restrictions on access imposed by streamside geology, Marty was having to learn how to cast weighted nymphs upstream and control their drift as the current carried them straight down at her.

I was on the other side of the river, wading in the shallows and fishing the edge of the current. I had given up trying to cast dry flies upstream while wading downstream. It took too much time and made my slick-soled wading too hazardous. So I was facing downstream, in the direction of travel, and casting across and down the current, letting the fly swing toward the shoalwater I was wading. I tried dead-drifting dry flies, letting them drown in the current, and it worked fine. So did wets, nymphs, and streamers. I was having a ball, catching one little rainbow after another. There wasn't much size to them—eight to twelve inches— but they were scrappy little devils. In Serbo-Croatian they are *Kalifornijska pastrmka,* California trout, genealogically accurate, but not nearly so apt as the Slovene name, *Sarenka,* which means multicolored. And these certainly were multicolored fish.

In one stretch of water here at the beginning of

the night jump—a stretch that covered considerably less than a quarter of a mile—the fish I caught ranged from pale silver to deeply hued and boldly marked, the stripe of color from the palest pastel pink to bright, fiery red. Whether these represented differences in age, sex, brood stocks, or breeding conditions I didn't know. But the variety was remarkable. I've never seen such color variation in the same species of approximately the same size in so short a stretch of water. I was having so much fun catching these little scrappers, I had lost track of time. It was getting late. I was in danger of dawdling.

Vojc and Ed were well out of sight and Marty had already moved into the stretch between the first and second bends downstream, where she was fishing while standing knee-deep in the water below a high, sandy bank. As I started downstream, I made one last cast out into the current ahead of me and to my left. As the fly—a Letort Hopper— began swinging across the current, the line stopped, then went taut. The rod bent over and the reel drag started slipping. This was no bitty 'bow.

So far on the trip, none of us had landed a big fish. Plenty of nice ones, yes, but nothing truly big.

The biggest trout any of us had taken so far had been about thirty-five to forty centimeters, fourteen to sixteen inches, and they had been browns. Our guides had taken bigger fish—that very morning, Vojc had taken three grayling bigger than that—but they carried nets and were more strongly motivated to keep fish. [Throughout Yugoslavia, an impoverished country by our standards, trout was typically the most expensive thing on the menu. Even more expensive than game meats like venison, bear, and wild boar.] None of us had bothered to carry a landing net, and we were releasing most of the fish we caught, anyway. [Now and then we kept a few to eat, and our Slovenian tourist guide was forever imploring us to keep some fish for him.] Several bigger fish had been hooked, but none landed, having been lost to the native ability of the fish to use the powerful resistance of the river currents, our lack of nets, and our willingness to accept what in the Florida Keys are called Palm Beach releases in favor of getting back into action on fresh adversaries.

The adversary I was battling certainly had the right moves. The fish had been downstream of me when I had hooked it, and it stayed downstream, running with the current, turning sideways to the current, working that stream to a fare-thee-well. I never got a good look at the fish during the fight. It splashed at the surface several times, but it never cleared the water in a jump. Whenever I let it run, it could take line off against the drag. But I could stop it by taking the line in my hand when I wanted to, which was often enough, there being a bit of a log jam at the constricted foot of the wide spot I was fishing. I didn't want to lose this fish to the downed trunks and branches before I got a good look at it. I don't like losing fish, especially unseen fish, and especially not when they give such a good account of themselves; it gives me a hollow, sick feeling in the pit of my much-abused stomach.

I don't know how long I fought this particular fish, but it seemed like a long time. I could stop him, but I couldn't gain much line on him against the current. The longer it lasted, the more I became convinced that this was a battle of strength, not weight. Whenever the fish paused, I could take line at will. His dead weight didn't offer that much resistance. But when the fish resumed the struggle, I stopped taking line. How much pressure could safely be put on the fine tippet or on the fish's mouth tissue? I knew I would release the fish if I could, if it weren't injured in some vital spot, but I had to get a good look at this one.

Finally, I maneuvered the fish into the

shallows and it was all over. After several abortive attempts—during which the fish almost made it back into deep water several times—I got my hand on the eye of the fly, which was hooked solidly in the corner of the jaw. I held the fish up to admire and inspect it. The fish seemed to be in fine shape for release. A gorgeous creature to be sure, this was an average-looking rainbow trout: its silvery body only moderately speckled, with a steely green back and a nice rosy flush down its flanks. Its proportions were about average, too, it being neither slender nor deep-bodied. There wasn't really anything about this fish to suggest why it had battled so fiercely and long. And it was only about ten inches long. What sporting genes this little guy had inherited!

The fish struggled to free itself as I struggled to get the fly unhooked from its jaw. When I lowered the unhooked fish into a little pool next to the shallows where I knelt, it swam away from my hands almost immediately. No need to revive this battler. No lingering fond farewells, either.

Before starting down toward Marty, who was almost out of sight around the second bend downstream, I inspected the fly. Or what was left of it. There wasn't much left, just the deer-hair head and some ragged yellow dubbing on the shank. And that was all. The rest of the hopper had been totally destroyed. I've seen flies survive better than this in the fearsome jaws of big chopper bluefish. How this little rainbow trout had managed to do such a terminal job on this fly, I will never understand but forever admire.

It was getting late and I had to fish the rest of the stretch down to the bridge in something like haste. A pity, because this was an enormously varied and complex river. This stretch of the Sava Bohinjka was unlike the other sections of the river we had fished previously, yet it possessed a wide variety of fishable water. Bottoms ranged from rock to gravel to sand to hard mud. There were deep, undercut banks, hummocking banks with over-hanging vegetation, and gravelly edgewater shoals. Runs, riffles, pockets, pools, eddies—it had them all. As well as plenty of trout. As I waded rapidly down the river toward our rendezvous, the water deepened and I caught many more browns than rainbows. I would love to devote three or four days to fishing this one stretch that we covered in less than two hours. Maybe some day I will.

After coming together at the bridge and trading a few stories, we hurried off to another part of the river, which we fished until nightfall. The river was wider and rockier than the sections we had already fished, yet the current was strong as ever. As soon as you got into water that was more than waist deep, you had to devote all your strength and attention merely to staying upright.

By the time darkness had fallen and the night jump was over, everyone had caught plenty of fish. Ed Ricciuti, who had been experiencing the most frustratingly bad luck all throughout the trip, was finally into one fish after another. His whoops and shouts must have been audible in nearby Austria and Italy. Some of the fish were landed—a few to be kept for the guides' families, and the rest to be released— but a lot more were released prematurely. Some big fish had been hooked, but none landed. The current claimed the lion's share of lip-hooked fish, but we also lost fish to rocks and haste and angler ineptitude, as well as to showing off. I had a particularly nice brown on for a long while, maybe eighteen inches long and a real jumper, but I tried jumping it one time too many for Jack's camera.

In the high-spirited gabble during the ride back to the Zlatorog that night, there was a lot of ribbing and kidding about big fish lost to lame brains and fumbling fingers. And there was much vying for honors of biggest fish landed, and of even bigger fish hooked and sighted, but lost. So many fish had been caught, no one minded the ones that had been lost. In some ways, they furnished the fodder for the best stories of all. We all had plenty of tales to tell and everyone seemed to be in the running for most and biggest fish.

But of all the dozens of fish I had hooked up with that night, the one I remember best and most fondly, the one I'd like most to tangle with again, was that ten-inch rainbow back at the beginning of the night jump. What a fish.

The Competitive Knot

By JAY H. CASSELL

T HAD BEEN a frustrating day. My good friend Gary, who'd come five hours from his home to test one of my favorite trout streams, had already taken six trout—all fat brownies, measuring from 15 to 22 inches—but I hadn't caught even one.

I always knew that Gary was a better fisherman than I. He has a bit more patience than I do, his knowledge of aquatic insects is as good as anyone's, and he seems to have that special knack— I won't call it luck—that always puts him in the right place at the right time. Still, the thought of being skunked on my stream in front of an old fishing buddy didn't please me at all.

I'd spent the day missing strikes, botching casts and generally getting quite infuriated at myself.

Finally, when I couldn't bear watching Gary's smooth casts any longer, I waded out of the stream, busted through the vegetation on the bank, and walked downstream.

After a few hundred yards, I came upon a section of stream where the water slowed into a wide turnpool, flowed through some riffles, and then widened out into a long, slow-moving flat. Looking downstream, I could see that the flat water eventually ran into some more riffles, then curved out of sight. I figured I could hike downstream to the far riffles, then work my way up the slow section to the turnpool. I have to get into some trout in there somewhere, I reasoned. Even one medium-sized fish would make me feel better.

As I trudged through the undergrowth and mud, I reflected on how I'd hyped this stream to Gary for years. During a recent phone conversation, I'd finally persuaded him to drive the five hours to my house so we could fish together for the weekend. After an evening of bringing each other up-to-date on our lives, we had gone to sleep, arisen at dawn, then driven to the river.

The stream is tough to fish. Located about an hour north of New York City, it receives more than its share of angling pressure during the course of the season. The resident brown trout, protected by a one-14-inch-fish-per-day limit, are fat, big and as wary as they come. One poor cast, one false movement in the water, and you put them down.

It was August, and most of the mayfly hatches had come and gone. To catch trout now, minuscle dry flies or nymphs are about your only hope. At the moment, I had on a small cream variant that I had selected after losing a No. 20 black ant to an unforgiving tree limb. Gary hadn't changed flies all day.

When I reached the downstream riffles, I sat down on a big rock, pulled out my pipe and had a smoke. I was daydreaming more than analyzing the water when I heard an unmistakable *plop* in the water just upstream of the riffles. *Plop.* There it was again.

On the far side of the stream, about eight yards away, a trout was steadily rising to some caenis flies that were coming off the water. I watched, fascinated, as the brown trout—and he was a big one, no question—came up every twenty seconds with clocklike precision. He was right next to the bank, just behind a small clump of grass sticking out of the water. An easy cast, I thought, until I noticed the low-hanging branch just four inches over his lie.

The only way I can get a cast in there is to

place my fly within inches of that clump of grass. Then, if I let my fly float down under the branch, he can't miss it.

This is it, I thought. God, he's big.

I put out my pipe, placed it into the breast pocket of my vest, got down on my knees and crawled over the shoreline rocks. When I was within casting range, I paused for another look. *He has to go 24 inches, maybe more. Maybe he wandered up from the reservoir just recently. He hasn't seen me. He's still rising.*

I looked behind me, saw an opening in the trees where my backcast wouldn't snag, and began to false cast. *One, two, three.* I came forward on the cast and shot the fly toward the grass clump.

Things happened so rapidly that I reacted on instinct more than reason. The cast was perfect, one of the best I've ever made. The little cream variant settled on the water not one inch from the edge of the grass clump. *Take that, Gary.* The fly was immediately picked up by the current and floated directly under the overhanging branch. There was that telltale *plop* as the brown swam forward, sucked in my offering, and started to submerge once again.

As soon as I saw the rise, I raised my rod tip sharply, pulled in line with my left hand, and got up

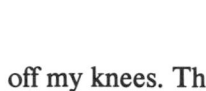

off my knees. The fish panicked and rushed into the middle of the stream, where he went deep. I could feel a tremendous weight on the end of my line. I kept my rod tip high, applied just enough pressure to keep the fish from running down over the riffles and . . . without warning, the line snapped.

I stood there, staring at the water. The whole thing couldn't have lasted ten seconds. Then, downstream, just above the riffles, a huge trout— had to have gone twenty-six inches—hurtled out of the water, crashed back down, and then was gone. *Stupid angler, you've got your nerve.*

I reeled in my line and mused over what had happened. In my frenetic frustration earlier in the day, I kept hanging up in the trees and in my haste to catch a fish, to compete with Gary, I had neglected to inspect my tippet. Too busy. Holding it in my hand now, I could see two windknots just above where the line had snapped. There obviously had been a third.

I waded to the rock, pulled out my pipe and had another smoke. A long smoke. Nowadays, I prefer to fish on my own when I can. It has nothing to do with Gary or anyone else. The fact is, I work hard all week and usually end up fishing only on weekends. Work is competition, not necessarily with your fellow workers, but with the job. But fishing, that shouldn't be competition. It should be relaxing and not competition against anyone but yourself. If you start to feel that you're competing against other fisherman, your fishing efficiency won't be what it should be.

I haven't let a windknot slip by unnoticed since then, either.

Floating the
Wild Rogue

By **MARTY SHERMAN**

HERE ARE TIMES when a fishing trip becomes something more than being out on the water after fish. These are the times when close companionship combines with perfect weather, a river of exceptional scenic beauty, and willing fish to make an experience that, as it is happening, you know is a thing of remarkable rarity. In October of 1981 I was fortunate enough to be a part of such a total fishing experience.

My father and I have a custom of spending a week fishing together in the fall each year. Dad has been a resident of Alaska, where I was raised, since 1948, and sometimes it is hard for him to leave when the Cold Bay goose shooting is just getting good. Nevertheless, he faithfully makes his southerly fall migration each year to fish with his eldest son. Usually we spend our time roaming and casting the banks of the Deschutes River. In 1981, however, I had a new suggestion: We should float the thirty-four mile wild and scenic section of the Rogue River. We would be floating with my friend Stan Jacobs, who spends as much time floating wild rivers as many professional guides and more than some. Rounding out the personnel for the trip would be Joyce Findley, giving us two people per boat. Perhaps part of the reason that trip is so memorable to me is that Miss Findley later became my wife.

Our put-in-point, the one most frequently used for this float, was at Grave Creek. That is a pretty grim-sounding place to begin a journey through more than eighty mild to major rapids, but nearly every portion of the wild and scenic section of the Rogue has some type of historical significance and has been named accordingly. Grave Creek is one example: It is the gravesite of an early settler. Other examples are China Gulch, a mining area worked by Chinese; and Rainie Falls, where a man named Rainie speared salmon for the commercial market. This historical identification is part of the Rogue River's charm. As we floated the calm water between rapids and in camp we could refer to our river guidebook for significant information about the section we were passing.

Our first morning on the water plunged us downriver into the heart of the canyon. A short float beyond Grave Creek Rapids is Rainie Falls. At this point hard boats must be lined through a smaller, less hazardous channel. The main waterfall is avoided by nearly all boaters, except those certain few rafters with an acute case of bravado. The middle chute is, however, negotiable in a large heavy-duty raft. Stan took my Dad through—they looked like a couple of rodeo riders taking on a bull in tandem.

All morning a lid of clouds had covered the canyon's ridges, and just above Wildcat Rapids we decided to take advantage of this favorable condition and do some fishing. Having only fished the Rogue once before this trip, I am far from being an expert on the river or the fly fishing techniques that it demands. The popular technique seems to include the use of full sinking lines cast quartering downstream. Guides use the full sinking or sink tip lines and keep their clients in the driftboats as they troll them back and forth across a productive piece of water. Rafts such as the ones we used for our trip do not lend themselves to this style of fishing. They are just too hard to hold against the current. For our fishing we let Stan's previous experience and the angling classic by Clark Van Fleet, *Steelhead To A Fly,* be our guide. We used double taper and weight-forward floating lines with flies in the six and eight size range.

Dad and Stan had beached their raft on the upper tip of an island in midstream. Stan began to work the smaller channel near the bank, while Dad started in the main stream of the river. Joyce and I had beached on the south bank and were a little slower getting our rods put together. As we threaded leader through the guides we stole glances across at Stan and Dad. In near unison their rod tips bowed and the clicking of reel ratchets could be heard over the throaty rumble of the river. As though we were viewing some kind of carnival magician's show, bolts of silver appeared and disappeared above and below the river's glassy surface. It wasn't long until Joyce and I too felt the tug and run of the Rogue's "little bolts of silver."

For an hour we stayed and fished this pleasant, productive stretch of river. For a good portion of that time several guide boats worked the water above us. Once I overheard a client ask his guide enviously, "Can we get on the bank and fish like those people?" We smugly continued to hook fish.

One of the guide's clients pulled out a movie camera to photograph Joyce and me. That was enough for that guide: He let the current carry his boat over the lip of the tailout and into Wildcat's churning rapids. The client craned his neck around for some final footage while I watched with apprehension as the bobbing boat disappeared around the corner where I would soon have to follow.

The necessity to move downriver to our first scheduled camp spot brought an end to our fishing earlier than we would have liked, but we still had the camp water to look forward to.

The rapids we encountered on our way to our first campsite near the Telephone Hole provided as much excitement as the fish and, for this novice boatman, plenty of dread. Upper and Lower Black Bar, Slim Pickens, Plow Share and Horseshoe Bend rapids are a few. All were negotiated safely, and the experience I gained had helped to build my confidence in my ability with the oars.

The campsite was reached with time enough to set up tents, put together the kitchen area and then get in a couple more hours of fishing. Dad was the most successful that evening. He worked slowly and carefully through a piece of calm water at the Telephone Hole. Casting a small Juicy Bug on an eight-foot rod with double taper six floating line, he landed and released fish after fish that evening. Finally, out of revenge I think, one of the spunky little pugilists took his now tattered Juicy Bug away from him. "It will take awhile to get another fly so well seasoned," I jokingly told Dad.

That evening, after darkness had ended our fishing, something happened that would cool our hot streak of fishing for a couple of days. While cooking our evening meal by lantern light we becme aware of a subtle change in the sound of the river. Flashlight beams were cast in the river's direction, and we saw our rafts, once pulled up dry, were now afloat. We pulled them up on dry rocks again and tethered the ropes to objects further up the beach. In the next hour and thirty minutes we repeated this process three times. Slowly the water crept to within a few feet of our kitchen, and then it seemed to stabilize. We marked the high-water line with rocks. By morning the river was back down to normal, and the rafts had to be dragged back down to the water. I feel sorry for anyone who might have been camping down close to the river's edge that night.

The reason for the sudden rise in the water was the draining of an upriver reservoir. To me it seems that this was done in a foolish, inconsiderate, potentially dangerous manner. We estimated that the river's volume increased by one-third to one-half. That is a lot of water to put into the river without prior warning. The raised water level did not pose any threat to our party, nor did we hear of any group having trouble with it. What it did, however, was put the fish off the bite for nearly forty-eight hours. Every boat that came past said the same thing—fishing had turned sour. The river carried a burden of suspended sediment; our best angling efforts went unrewarded.

Wednesday morning came, and it was time to move downriver to our next campsite. As we approached Battle Bar the scene was so tranquil we felt compelled to stay just for the sheer beauty of the place. Autumn colors dominated the river's banks. Oaks, maple and vine maple were reflected on the water's broad, flat surface and leaves slipped singly from their branches in a last brief ballet as their season reached its end. We knew that this warm, inviting place must be enjoyed.

Our fishing was sporadic and only fair at best. The river was clearing more each day, yet the fish remained unresponsive. But the season and the river held us captive in relaxed contentment. We sat peacefully at the water's edge and considered how fifty and sixty years ago people like Prince Helfrich, Zane Grey, and Glen Wooldridge floated and fished this river. Our two nights at Battle Bar passed too quickly. It was with much regret that we loaded our rafts and started downriver.

Winkle Bar was not far downriver, and we stopped there to walk around the old Zane Grey property. A brief try with the fly rods here brought us four or five nice half-pounders, and we all began to think in terms of serious fishing again. With this encouragement our downstsream progress became a bit hastier.

Just ahead lay Mule Creek Canyon and Blossom Bar. Although I had been a passenger through both the previous year and Stan had thoroughly coached me on how to negotiate their corkscrew, piledriver currents, I was still nervous as hell. Up came "The Jaws" of Mule Creek. We maneuvered to the correct approach position and dropped into the abyss, Stan far ahead, with me straining to watch every part of the river and trying to follow Stan's watery path down the rock-bound river. It came off without a hitch; I kept the rafts straight all through the canyon and hardly brushed the wall. The credit for such a clean run clearly goes to the lightweight, very maneuverable raft I was rowing. The balance and design of Willie Illingsworth's River Rat rowing frames were great factors in helping this greenhorn boatman make a safe trip.

What makes Mule Creek Canyon such an awesome piece of water? Just this: The Rogue here has sliced its way through solid rock, choking the entire river down through a deep, narrow passage, sometimes only fourteen or fifteen feet wide, with some terrific hydraulics. One place in the canyon known as the Coffeepot has held boats for ten or twenty minutes. Occasionally another boat will come into the Coffeepot before the previous boat can break free of its hydraulic grip, and they become engaged in a weird game of bumper boats until the river decides they have had enough and serves them their release.

I cannot describe the beauty of Mule Creek Canyon appropriately. It is rock, and water, and a cool silence that demands respect, even reverence. Going through it only once will rivet the place in your memory. Going through the second time makes you ask how you could remember so little of its awesomeness.

Blossom Bar demands the utmost respect also. Blossom is a rock garden. We scouted it. Stan explained it. Then we ran it, Stan first, with me following five frightened minutes later. I made it through without any problem; I felt great. I'm a hot dog white-water boater! Now I look at the slides that Joyce took as I went through and I can see how wrong I had the boat positioned a couple of times and how lucky I am that the boat responded so well to the urging of the oars as rocks loomed up in my path.

Our last night was spent at Brushy Bar. We all wished it could be five more days instead of being the last. Below Blossom power boats are permitted, and there was a guide using a jet boat near our camp who seemed to stay just ahead of me as I tried to get to a run downriver. I decided to play the fish catching game from behind him, on the bank, as he trolled flies at midstream. After I hollered the fifth "Fish on!" whoop he drove on downstream, his two round clients staring back upstream, fishless, as number five shot into the air.

In camp that evening we were visited by three deer. They sampled a bar of soap, then settled for leftover salad. They were the finest dinner guests, politely stepping behind our chairs, accepting everything we offered, and grateful for a second helping.

We made one long float to our termination point on the last day. We fished briefly in the morning and ironically the fish that were so cooperative for me the previous evening shunned

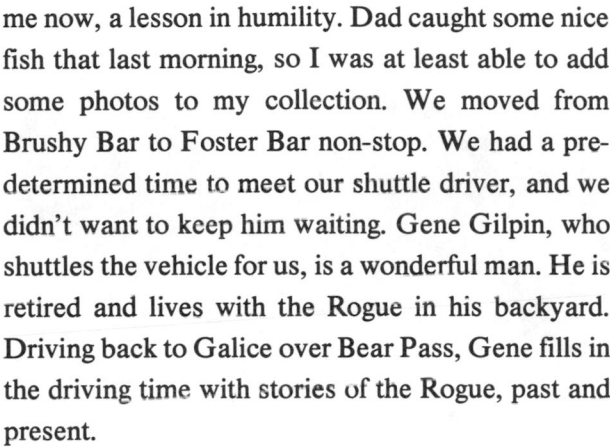

me now, a lesson in humility. Dad caught some nice fish that last morning, so I was at least able to add some photos to my collection. We moved from Brushy Bar to Foster Bar non-stop. We had a pre-determined time to meet our shuttle driver, and we didn't want to keep him waiting. Gene Gilpin, who shuttles the vehicle for us, is a wonderful man. He is retired and lives with the Rogue in his backyard. Driving back to Galice over Bear Pass, Gene fills in the driving time with stories of the Rogue, past and present.

We all regretted that our trip had come to an end, but we laughed as we recounted the events of the past week. It was my Dad who made the boldest statement, especially when you consider his years of fishing and hunting in Alaska: "That is the best trip I've ever made." We all looked at each other and smiled and began to make plans for next year.

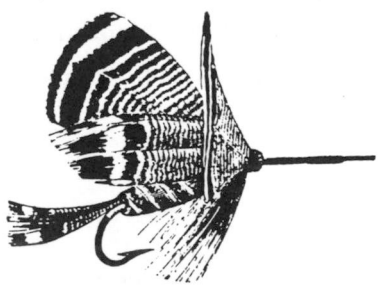

I Remember Barnegat

By **VIN T. SPARANO**

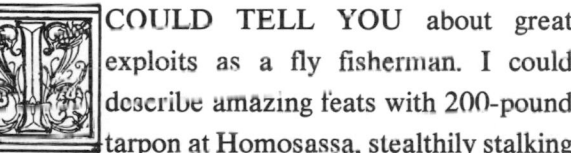COULD TELL YOU about great exploits as a fly fisherman. I could describe amazing feats with 200-pound tarpon at Homosassa, stealthily stalking bonefish on the Bahamian flats, or battling broad-backed trout in Argentina . . . but I'm sorry to say that none of those things have ever happened to me. Please don't misunderstand. I have fished for tarpon, bonefish and trout with a fly rod. It's just that trying to relive certain fly fishing memories can be painful.

I would prefer to talk about how I was introduced to fly fishing nearly thirty years ago. I was out of college only about a year or so when *Outdoor Life* magazine hired me as an Associate Editor. Even though I grew up in Newark, New

Jersey, I still thought I knew a lot about hunting and fishing. Every chance I had I spent in the woods or on some stream somewhere. When I wasn't in the field I was reading the outdoor magazines, especially columns by such legends as Ray Bergman, Jack O'Connor, Jason Lucas, Joe Brooks and other giants in the field. So when Bill Rae, the Editor-in-Chief at that time, sent me to Tom's River, New Jersey, to take part in the first official meeting of the Salt Water Flyrodders of America, I welcomed the chance to show my stuff. But then I found out that some of the attendees were the very same legends I had been reading about for years. I suddenly got very weak in the knees.

It was a chilly April afternoon when I walked out on that dock in Tom's River back in 1960. A group of fishermen were watching this short guy fly cast and spout the virtues of a fiberglass fly rod that he helped design. I wasn't much impressed with his sales pitch, but he amazed me with his casting. He would double-haul a few times, then shoot out about one-hundred feet of line. When all the loose coils at his feet finally sailed through the guides, the line would snap taut like a banjo string. When he had a good-sized audience, he took just the tip section of his two-piece fly rod and continued to double-haul and shoot out sixty to eighty feet of line. Then, using

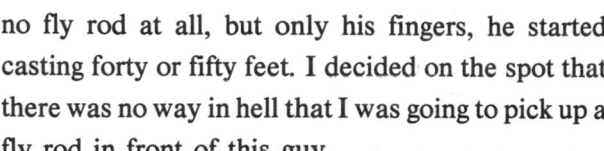

no fly rod at all, but only his fingers, he started casting forty or fifty feet. I decided on the spot that there was no way in hell that I was going to pick up a fly rod in front of this guy.

I soon discovered that this great fly caster was Lefty Kreh, an expert I had been reading about for years. Naturally, Lefty made me nervous, but meeting the rest of the men on that dock really did me in. Frank Woolner, one of the pioneers at *Salt Water Sportsman,* shook my hand and led me over to Lefty who was wrapping up his demonstration. Lefty was so excited about his new fly rod that he shoved it at me and said, "Here, try it. The rod is perfect."

So there I was. I held a ten-foot Fenwick in my hand with about 100 feet of fly line coiled at my feet. I looked out at the water and suddenly realized that I was staring at whitecaps and the wind was biting into my cheeks. I knew I had bought the farm. But what the hell. I stripped in all but thirty feet, picked up the line in one clean move, kept my backcast high and drove the rod forward in a powerful cast. I don't really know what happened next, except that even today I realize how lucky I was that I did not have a big 2-0 Honey Blonde tied to that tippet. When I finished peeling the loops of fly line and backing from around my head, neck and shoulders, I looked up and saw Lefty standing there. Probably for the first and last time in his life Lefty Kreh was speechless. Finally, he said, "I think I know what you're doing wrong." He was being kind.

When most of the outdoor press had retreated to the bar, which is usually where you'll find most of the outdoor press, Lefty stayed on the dock and gave me fly casting lessons—the first I'd ever had in my life. He showed me the mechanics of the cast, which I have never forgotten. But timing, Lefty said, is the key to good fly casting. According to Lefty, my timing would come later. I have to confess that my timing never did improve a great deal, but I did learn to drive a big fly out a respectable distance without injury to myself or anyone around me. I have Lefty to thank for that.

The following day turned out beautiful. The wind layed down, which it rarely does when I go fishing. The tide was just right and I knew we'd find some striped bass on the Barnegat Bay flats behind Island Beach State Park. I knew I could catch them on a casting rod with a Rebel plug, but now I had to use a fly rod, which would be no small obstacle for me and my newly acquired skill. But I was determined to give it my best. Once out on the water I knew I would be comfortable with a fly rod because I would be away from the critical eyes of guys like Kreh, Woolner and that new show-off Mark Sosin, who was no older than me. How did he learn to use a fly rod so quickly?

Just when I was beginning to feel more confident, I met my partner for the day and I started to get the queasies all over again. I'd be sharing a boat with Joe Brooks, the guy I used to watch on the "American Sportsman" television show every Sunday afternoon. Brooks was a celebrity and he never did anything wrong in a boat. I was in real trouble now.

As I recall, our guide for the day was a young local fisherman named George and he was ecstatic about takng someone like Joe Brooks fishing. Here was the famous fisherman George saw on television. Brooks was also the fishing editor of *Outdoor life* and lots more. But I could immediately tell that George wasn't too excited about the prospect of having me aboard. He didn't really know who I was and I could tell that he didn't much care.

George put Brooks in the bow of the boat so that he would have plenty of casting room. George sat in the stern of the big outboard boat, which left me the middle seat with not a lot of room to control my casting so that I wouldn't hurt anyone, including myself. I cleverly decided to keep my embarrassment to a minimum, so I pretended to spend a few minutes checking over my Honey Blonde and leader knots. I wanted Brooks to cast first, hoping he would get too busy to notice me. I didn't really care whether I caught a striper. I just wanted to do some decent casting in front of these two guys. I tried to remember what Lefty taught me the day before. God, if I could cast like that! I imagined shooting more than 100 feet of fly line and backing through the guides, watching all those coils unravel at my feet and the line snapping tight like a garter belt.

So I toyed with my rod and watched Brooks out of the corner of my eye. What was this? No double-haul? After a few false casts, he let his balsa popper set down right over a drop off at the edge of the flats no more than thirty or forty feet from the boat. He popped the popper a few times, the water exploded and Joe was fast into a nine or ten-pound striper that he landed and carefully released.

Joe began casting again and all his casts were the same. He rarely double-hauled. There was no need to build up all that power into his casts. Joe was more concerned about getting his popper in the right spot where he knew the stripers would be feeding. Our boat would occassionally put us into the wind, forcing Joe to shoot out a more powerful cast. He knew how to cast well into his fly line backing, and didn't knock himself out with long casts because he knew where the fish were. We could reach them easily.

Joe caught about a dozen stripers that day and I even picked up a few. It didn't matter that my double-haul was awful. I knew I could catch fish anyway. Joe explained that understanding structure and fish habits were more important than firing out a long cast. He proved it that day ... and I proved it to myself when I caught a few stripers with my awkward casting. But as Joe explained later there are times when you are forced into situations where you will have to get out that long line. The point he proved, though, is that you don't have to be a master of the fly rod to catch fish.

Over the years, Joe, Lefty and I became good friends. I have fished and worked with both men and I enjoyed every minute of it. Joe posed for all the fly casting photos in my *Complete Outdoors Encyclopedia*. At one point in our careers, Lefty became *Outdoor Life's* fishing editor and I had many opportunities to get into the field with him. Joe, unfortunately, is no longer with us. But Lefty and I are still around to relive the old times.

I'll never forget those days with Lefty and Joe on Tom's River nearly thirty years ago. I learned a lot from my two friends. Whenever I pull off a good cast with a fly rod, I know I'm using some of the techniques that Lefty showed me. I still see Lefty often, but I don't think I've reminded him lately of our first encounter so long ago. I should thank him again. I really think Lefty knows down deep that you don't really have to be a great caster with a fly rod to catch fish, but Lefty enjoys demonstrating those unbelievable casts, so his secret is safe with me.

I wish I could have fished more often with Joe Brooks, but it just wasn't to be. Joe's death was sudden and a great loss to all of us who knew him. I'll always remember Joe catching those stripers on those short little casts with a balsa popper that still bears his name. Joe read the water. He knew the fish were there. He didn't have to drive out 100 feet of line to catch those fish and he knew it.

I learned a lot from Lefty and Joe, and will always be grateful to them. My hope is that someday I'll be able to repay them by helping some young fisherman who can't figure out where all the knots came from in his leader.

Baiting the Fly Trap

By ED GRAY

"RY FLY, wet fly. Who cares? Throw 'em some salami if it works."

Salami? This could be good. I stopped to listen; they didn't notice me.

"Look. The trout wants to eat a real bug, right?"

"Right."

"And if you put that actual bug on your hook, that's bait, right?"

"Right."

"So anything else that ain't the real bug, that's a fake, right?"

"Right."

"So what's a fake?"

"What's a *fake*?"

"Yeah. What's a fake?"

"Well, you just said . . ."

"An artificial."

"An . . . Yeah, okay."

"An artificial. Am I right?"

"Yeah. Right."

This *was* good. Two guys I didn't know, sitting at the lunch counter on a grey Tuesday in March. "Just coffee," I said. I could wait this one out. Socrates went on.

" 'Artificial Lures Only.' Give me a break."

" 'Artificial *Flies* Only' is going to be the rule."

"Yeah, I know. Sheee . . ."

"And catch-and-release, too."

A mumble from Socrates.

I knew what they were talking about: the new "quality-fishing" stretch on the Nipumet River. All the local bait fishermen and plug casters were opposed, of course; I had a few reservations myself.

Socrates was back on the podium:

"If we're gonna put 'em all back, who cares what we use to catch 'em?"

"Well . . ."

"Long as we don't hurt 'em."

"Yeah . . ."

"I mean, why not feed 'em some real food while we're playin' around with 'em."

"Well, yeah, but . . ."

"Ahh, come *on*. You mean you think we're doing a trout a big favor by letting him munch on old feathers stored in *moth* balls?"

"Now wait . . ."

"Dipped in *head* cement? You ever *sniff* that stuff?"

"Yeah. I mean no. But it's dried . . ."

"And then we what? Save the marshmallows for ourselves?"

Who was this guy? I ordered a doughnut, wondered if they had a flagon of hemlock in the back room, waiting.

"Okay, then," he went on. "Let me ask you this: A deer-hair mouse okay on that water?"

"Yeah, sure."

"That's an artificial fly, right?"

"Yeah. You know that. It's a classic."

"A classic. Yeah. Okay, okay then. Then do you have to use deer hair?"

"No. Of course not. That's just the name. You can use caribou or moose, I suppose. Deer hair works best, I think . . ."

"Can you use mouse hair?"

"*Mouse* hair?"

"Yeah."

"Well, it wouldn't float. It's not hollow."

"But you can use it."

"I guess so. Sure."

"Okay, how about I use a whole mouse?"

"No way. That's not a fly. That's bait."

"Oh. So the whole mouse is out, but the hair is okay."

"Yeah."

I felt like a kid in the movies, wanting to yell out, *Look out—Here it comes*! Socrates sat up straight on the stool:

"Okay, okay. I get a hook, spin on some mouse hair. It's okay, right?"

"Yep."

"And I tie in a little hackle, maybe some chenille, a strip of rabbit fur?"

"Might be lousy fly."

"But legal."

"Yeah."

"How about if I take out the hackle and the chenille and put in a *lot* of mouse fur?"

" . . . "

"How about I wrap a whole mouse fur around the hook? How about a stuffed mouse? How about a whole mouse without the formaldehyde?"

"Whoa. That just became bait."

"Bait."

I started to get up.

"Man, there are some weird guys making up these rules . . ."

Outside the sleet had started, but I felt warm and refreshed. The coffee had been good. I like a place that serves it with real cream.

A Distant Splash

By JOHN RANDOLPH

ETER SAT motionless, his eyes fixed on the pool by the cottonwood. In the gathering darkness a trout's black snout appeared and then disappeared at the edge of a swirl.

Peter shifted his weight from one cheek to the other. Things were about to happen predictably, he thought. He was, for once, on a roll—at the right place at the right time. He could, possibly, control things for a while.

Another, very large, very dark snout appeared ahead of the rise rings left by the first fish, and in a langorous side-to-side motion the trout's head began to feed. Peter eased his right hand, quivering, up and across his chest to his left ear and scratched where the mosquito had landed. This would be duck soup, he thought, nothing like Black Monday at the office, or his disintegrating marriage.

Quickly other snouts began to appear in the near darkness. The oil-like surface of the pool was all rise rings and trout noses, and above the water purple martins dove and pirhouetted to take the hatching mayflies.

With his left hand Peter eased open the zipper on his vest pocket and slid a fly box out onto his lap. "The right Christmas fishing gift for the right Dad," he recalled.

As usual, the box would not open easily. Peter squeezed it hard with two hands. Its plastic lips popped suddenly and its contents of flies sprang out and onto his lap.

Peter's hands quivered as he hurriedly retrieved the flies and returned them in clumps of twos and threes to the little plastic cubicles in the box. He could re-arrange them later back in the motel, he thought. The god-damned fly box had, like his marriage, never been quite right. When he needed it to perform, it had always failed.

The gentle slurp of a trout caught Peter's attention momentarily.

Why had he allowed the little, unimportant things to become the dominant forces in his life? Certainly the job had turned out badly, but perhaps he's expected too much of it. Perhaps if he'd become a corporate predator. Perhaps if he'd been the hunter he was in his youth. Perhaps it was the way he dressed for the office—the power clothing. Could it have been his body language? You can't advance up the corporate ladder without that tangible authoritative carriage—"command presence," they'd called it in officer's training.

When he'd returned the last fly to its compartment, Peter picked a delicate orange-bodied Hen Spinner and knotted it carefully to the thin tippet filament. He liked this part of the preparation for fishing. Each step in tying the knot was a meticulous ritual. A mistake could mean the loss of a trophy. It had been his continual mistakes with knots that had infuriated his father, who finally refused to fish with Peter "until you clean up your act."

Peter passed the monofilament through the eye of the hook twice, then wrapped it around the main strand six times and, before cinching it, gave it one last wrap for good measure. He examined the wraps to ensure that they did not overlap. He spit on them the way his father had. "That ought to fix him," he muttered, as the old man would have done standing in midstream and preparing for a big fish. Why, Peter wondered, could he not have been more like his father? He would easily have taken the big trout beside the cottonwood. And Dad would have whooped for all the river to hear when he hooked the "lunker." And all the office would have heard for months about "the old man's big trout," mounted on the wall, not to be touched by cleaning ladies, secretaries or "non-fishermen."

The big black head moved ponderously in the feeding current. Peter placed the fly box in its pocket and rose to a low crouch. If he could sneak down the bank below the trout, he could cast up to him. I'll have to be very careful with the cast, Peter thought. The line must sail in a tight loop to a point just below the trout, and the leader must fall so the tippet settles like a spider's filament on the fish's head. As the great snout wags in the current, with the tippet hanging on it, the fly will be drawn into the mouth. It will be a great sporting feat, something clean and successful to remember, to hoard as a private victory.

Peter slipped at the top of the bank and slid on his rump to the water's edge. The trout heads in the pool continued feeding, almost rhythmically. And the very large fish eased downcurrent slightly, toward Peter, to find a better eating place in the drifting flies.

"You greedy son-of-a-bitch; you've had the

radish," Peter muttered. This effort would be just like the old wing-shooting days, before Vietnam. He'd been a superb hunter.

To reach the trout for a proper fly presentation, Peter would have to wade the fast current at the tail of the pool. If I can reach the pool's tailout, he thought, I can make the cast up and over the head. It will be a long cast—perhaps fifty feet—but not beyond my ability. And if I make the cast, which will have to be made just right on the first sling, well, it will be something.

Peter tested the water gingerly. The stream bottom was slippery, and he could feel the rushing water tear at his legs as he moved foot by foot upstream toward the pool. I should have worn the stream cleats, he thought. With his left hand he felt his waistline for the waderbelt. "Damn!"

The fish rose rhythmically, confidently, in its new position. Peter inched closer by feeling boulders with his boot bottom, then wedging his foot sideways between them and hauling the down-stream foot up to the new position. He kept his body thin-side to the current to minimize drag. And with each move he stopped to watch the trout as it fed.

As he approached the trout, Peter's confidence grew. He'd never seen a trout quite that large. It would be a rainbow in this part of the river, he thought. Probably an old fish who dominated the pool with weight and karma.

The trout held in the pool's sweet spot, where the mayflies were swept into long, juicy eddy lines. "No wonder you're so fat and sassy," Peter whispered.

Close enough; don't push it, Peter thought.

He crouched at the lip of the pool and watched the fish's broad, flat nose come up. It lifted gently, creating no bow wave that might push away the weightless mayflies floating into its mouth. The fish lay suspended, head-up, its dorsal fin and tail obscured by the water. Only its great nose betrayed its true dimensions, like the head of a resting whale. It was a sight that Peter needed to see, and it held him spellbound in intense scrutiny of the head and its activity.

Peter's father would have called his first cast "a doozer." It shot tight-looped and straight in a clean line to where he wanted it to fall, below the feeding fish. But when the leader turned over in the air, the fly caught the line and the mess settled to the water.

"Shit!" Peter stood watching as the line floated downstream. The trout fed, undisturbed by the commotion behind it.

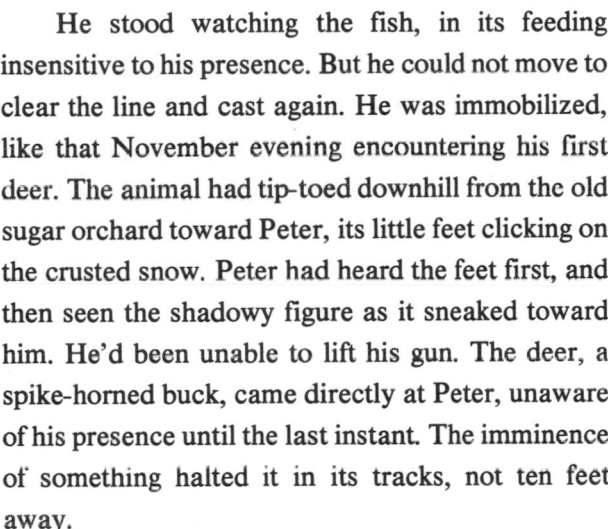

He stood watching the fish, in its feeding insensitive to his presence. But he could not move to clear the line and cast again. He was immobilized, like that November evening encountering his first deer. The animal had tip-toed downhill from the old sugar orchard toward Peter, its little feet clicking on the crusted snow. Peter had heard the feet first, and then seen the shadowy figure as it sneaked toward him. He'd been unable to lift his gun. The deer, a spike-horned buck, came directly at Peter, unaware of his presence until the last instant. The imminence of something halted it in its tracks, not ten feet away.

The buck had stared at Peter, trembling, then whirled and dashed away, its flag bobbing in the evening gloom. Five years later, when the Vietcong youth stumbled drunkenly into his night ambush, Peter had trembled, waiting until, at eight feet, the boy had suddenly felt the presence of death and halted. The burst from Peter's carbine had taken the boy in the chest, and he had died screaming. In the morning Peter photographed the body. Back home, he had shown the snapshots to friends, and even to strangers. Later he burned them.

Peter slowly retrieved the line and carefully untangled the fly and leader. The trout fed on, just visible now in the water's surface glare. He blew on the fly and dressed it lightly with floatant. Then he greased the leader out to the fly and reeled the line in until about thirty feet remained beyond the rod tip. This he cast into the air and waved to and fro until he had the feel of the line's weight down the rod into his hand. As he cast back and forth, he gradually worked more line into the air. He watched the line and fly as it snaked out nearer and nearer to the fish.

When the fly was over the fish, Peter released the two feet of line in his left hand and the line settled behind the trout. The fly landed with a tiny splash in the surface glare. At the same instant the snout came up and Peter lifted the rod tip gently and stripped the line smoothly with his left hand, the way his father had instructed. He felt weight.

The trout resisted the pressure but did not move. Perhaps it's never been hooked before, Peter thought. He reeled in until the line went tight and then lifted the rod gently. The great fish suddenly surged upstream toward the cottonwood. But as it bore into the pool's deeps, something splashed at the base of the tree and the trout, apparently frightened, turned and fled downstream directly at Peter.

"Here he comes!"

As Peter turned to avoid the fish, his foot

caught between the stones and the current took him flush and he felt himself spun slowly, uncontrollably. As he turned, he bent at the waist and sat into the water. "Just don't panic," he heard himself say as the icy chill of river water entered his beltless waders and shot down his legs. "Keep your feet pointed downstream and ride it out." He held the rod tip high, and he could feel the weight of the trout as it ran line. It was still running as Peter was swept away.

He knew he could float for several minutes, and he thought he would make shore before he sank. He was wrong, of course, and when he hit bottom and could not rise again, he struggled hard to find footing. The current tumbled him and, try as he might, he could not, in the speeding current, drive his feet down to thrust himself upward to the surface for air. After his third desperate try he gulped water. Then Peter panicked, thrashing upward desperately with both arms and legs, the rod still clutched in his right hand.

How far he drifted he could not know. He was on bottom now, and suddenly, the face of the Vietcong boy appeared to him and his father's voice said with great emphasis and clarity, "You're a nice guy, Peter, but you're a loser."

Peter's first attempt at crawling on bottom

moved him no more than a foot. But it had worked. By crawling and thrusting with his feet and grabbing and pulling with his hand, he could move in the direction of shallow water. He strained to prevent the current from tumbling him, and as he thrust himself forward, he felt the pressure of water ease. I must be in a pool, he thought.

His panic had nearly disappeared and a feeling of wonderful lassitude swept over him, and although he could not breath, he relaxed and floated— strangely, almost dreamily, in slow motion.

His head bumped something, and the word "loser" came to him through the dream. Peter lifted his left arm and his hand felt cold. Then it touched something—a rock—and Peter grasped it hard and pulled and thrust with his feet and legs. His head broke water and he gasped and thrust again hard. His chest came up on sand and he coughed water and gasped again. Peter heaved until the water vomited from his lungs. He rested with his chin on sand. He lifted his head slowly, but a convulsion of coughing forced his head down once more. He breathed spasmodically and waited.

By thrusting repeatedly with his feet and legs, Peter inched his way up the sand beach until he could turn over on his back and lift his legs. As he lifted, water rushed from his waders, spilling out onto the sand around his head and shoulders.

As he was about to make an attempt at rising, Peter felt a tug at his right hand. He still clutched the rod, the reel clean of line to the spool. The rod tugged; the trout was still on.

Lying prone on the sand, Peter reeled the yielding fish in slowly until its head appeared alongside him, its vermillion gill-cover stripe irridescent in the luminescent darkness. The fish listed slightly, righted itself and tilted again in its exhaustion.

Peter slowly passed the rod from his right to his left hand and gently grasped the fish and righted it. The trout lay quietly accepting Peter's ministrations. Its gill covers pulsed spasmodically.

Peter raised himself to an elbow and watched the fish for a moment. Then he heaved himself to a sitting position and cradled it in the water between his legs and gently removed the hook from its jaw. He held the head so the streaming water flowed into the fish's mouth and over its gills and measured the fish carefully with three spans of his fingers. "Twenty-seven inches."

He watched vibrant colors return to the fish's palid body. When the trout moved its spine in a first attempt at swimming in place, Peter released it. It sank slowly to bottom, holding itself there in the current beside him.

"Wait a little, fish," he said. "You got nothin' but time."

The trout moved and Peter almost reached to grab it before it could escape. It seemed to move without swimming, fading in to the darkness of the pool. Peter stared where it had been, but he could see nothing. Somewhere upriver there was a distant splash, and he rose and stepped off to hunt its maker.

A Pilgrim Among Alaskan Rainbows

By **PETER BARRETT**

LL RAINBOWS are alike, you say? Once, in youthful ignorance, I thought so too. Raised in the Northeast where rainbow trout were not all that plentiful then, I took my share and thought them nothing special. Wet and dry flies, streamers, spinners—anything worked.

Not until I made a trip to Alaska did I learn that rainbows can be damnably difficult—until one chances upon what the fish want.

Three friends and I had taken an airline fishing package to the Bristol Bay area the last week in May. We were at a camp handy to the falls on the Brooks River where brown bears feast on migrating salmon every summer. Only about two miles long, the Brooks is also well known for its rainbow fishing.

You could walk slowly along the bankside bear trails, worn deep above the falls, and glimpse rainbows up to eight or nine pounds finning in a couple of feet of ultraclear water. The adrenalin rush you feel at such sights is incredible. First you are paralyzed, afraid even to blink in case it might spook one of these giants.

But when you stand still as a tree, the trout ignore you and give the appearance of hungry fish. Occasionally one nips a passing morsel or tips down for something on the bottom.

Inevitably you back slowly away until distant enough to enter the river below a marked fish or two without panicking them. Then the bent-over upstream stalk. And, finally, the presentation of a wet fly or nymph on a fairly fine tippet, cast perhaps ten feet above the fish; the tense wait; and at last the payoff—bolting rainbows humping the water above their shoulders. A bullet in their midst couldn't have provoked wilder flight.

But a little No. 12 fly? It was maddening.

For three days we worked on the brutes we could see and cast for others invisible in the big falls pool. And we made the bitter discovery that we weren't good enough to take them, though we did well with the grayling.

Late on the last afternoon before moving to

another camp I came upon a dead rainbow of about three pounds which had drifted against the bank. I got in the river to examine him and noticed a wisp of leader trailing from its jaws. Lodged in the trout's throat was a big black fly, which I took.

The fly had a couple of rubber "legs" tied in at the head, plump black chenille body, short red tail, and a wing tight to the back of dark-brown straight hair. Back at the cabin I said, "Here's what they're taking," and threw the fly on the table.

Laughter. Disbelief. Scorn even.

But after dinner that night I saw a box of identical flies at the little tackle counter and bought the lot.

The next day we took a floatplane to Nonvianuk Lake for our final assault on the rainbows at its outlet, which is the start of the Alagnak River. That first morning after crossing the lake the pilot had a little problem with bank ice near the river, but managed to get us close enough to wade ashore. I was last out and asked the pilot what they were taking. "Anything big and black on the surface," he said with a grin. "I'll be back in eight hours."

Notice that I have plunged right into the fishing with scarcely a mention of the country? Alaska does that to you, especially the first time. Maybe it's the

chance to catch large trout that grabs you, yet being
in a fabled place has a magic of its own.

Consider the long days this far north. You can
fish—here we go again!—for several hours with
time out for lunch and dinner, yet still the sun hasn't
set, and if you have the strength, you can have at
'em again. This was when we enjoyed grayling on
dry flies on the Brooks River.

Though it was almost June, it felt and looked
like the beginning of spring in Connecticut. A
weather-beaten cabin in good repair stood at the
head of the Alagnak, which then was 46 degrees and
not too high to wade partway in. The endless sun
beat down. And wherever I looked it seemed
vaguely familiar, until I looked up at the sur-
rounding snow-capped mountains, gaudy as
postcards—a constant reminder that I was in a land
unlike any other.

Perhaps I drank all this in because I didn't want
to begin another fishless day. No glad cries drifted
from the river as I waded in and cast the big black fly
that I had removed from the dead rainbow. As the
fly floated I yanked hard to sink it. With a splash a
rainbow grabbed it and ran like hell down the
river.

Now it was a super day. I had to chase the trout
to a distant bend pool, stumbling along under the

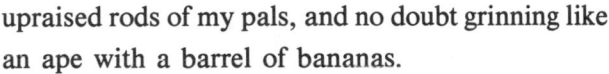

upraised rods of my pals, and no doubt grinning like an ape with a barrel of bananas.

Soon I broke out the box of flies. This black thing was just what the trout wanted, and *nothing else* [we were to find]. Why we hadn't asked anyone at Brooks I can't imagine. We thought we knew it all, I guess.

All this was before the time of the Woolly Bugger, leech flies, and such. No doubt Alaskans knew the score along with Western steelheaders, but the big rush from the Lower Forty-Eight was just building.

That day became an incredible circus. The trout ranged from just under three pounds, by our estimate, to about seven [kept for a wall mount]. Trout by the uncounted dozens were eager takers of the big black flies. All others, including some Atlantic salmon patterns, were ignored.

Next day the same. However, by the third and last day fishing was off drastically. No front was passing through. No change in the endless sun. As Bob Foreman remarked, "We've educated too many of them."

As my wandering increased I became more acquainted with big-river rainbows, yet the black Alaskan fly [though I tried it when fishing was slow in some rivers] didn't provoke rainbows in New

Zealand or Argentina, nor in British Columbia.

However, when I returned to Alaska on a spring bear hunt there it was again, a hankering for a big dark fly fished deep. This was east of Port Heiden on the Peninsula. I'd brought a fly-rod outfit, just in case, and an icy creek near camp yielded a few hefty rainbows. The trout were so sluggish they'd take only when the fly was barely moving, as on a discouraged, frozen-fingered reel-in.

They'd ignored all bright steelhead patterns and a few darkish ones like the Skunk. Finally I'd made a long dark fly from materials around camp: lead fuse wire for weight, hair from a ratty mink pelt, unraveled dark-gray wool from my hunting pants.

This they took, but why? *Because it was dark and twice the size of the steelhead flies?* I began to wonder.

Away from Alaska I caught rainbows on whatever turned them on, commonly flies resembling aquatic insects. The late-summer grasshopper season was the sole exception, especially in Western rivers.

And so the couple of black Alaskans remained unused in a fly box for years . . .

Another time I went to Alaska to fish for

rainbows out of Branch River Lodge. I was, of course, loaded with big black flies, weighted and unweighted, in modern patterns—black Woolly Buggers with and without sparkles of Flashabou, black leech flies, black Muddlers, and some huge hairy monsters of my own tying that resembled a spaced-out Woolly Worm on a stout 3-0 hook.

I could hardly wait to splat down a big black fly as we headed upstream on Branch River and onto the Alagnak whose top end I'd fished and mentioned earlier. Presently, guide Andy Owens swung into a channel, where we transferred to another aluminum boat with jet drive.

An hour later Andy beached the boat and we'd separated to fish. None of the black flies I tried brought so much as a follow. Meanwhile two Californians who had joined us this day—Lee Sager and Curt Longenecker—had rainbows splashing all over the river 100 yards downstream from me. So I waded down to find out what they were doing right.

"They're still feeding on salmon eggs," Lee Sager explained, holding up a short-shanked fly with a pink ball of fluff. "Any fly with a hot red or pink body might work. We think our single-eggers are better."

He gave me one and three split shot to pinch on

the leader about a foot above the fly. Because of the shot, you have to lob each cast. Then the current seizes and you feel a fast bump, bump, bump, for here the bottom was cobbled with small round rocks.

Presently, one of these bumps didn't feel right and I raised the rod. A rainbow's sudden energy jolted up the line as he took off. . . .

I was to learn what many Westerners have long taken for granted—salmon spawn, even old and pale, draws rainbows and grayling like nothing else. In late August throngs of salmon in a river tend to spook large rainbows and cause them to seek temporary havens in deep water where they may be difficult to rouse.

I also learned that rivers like the Alagnak don't have a wide variety of live forage for rainbows. There are no crawfish, no wide variety of minnows. Mayflies, small caddisflies, and stoneflies are scarce, and there are no grasshoppers. But there are sculpins and salmon and trout fry. Small rainbows and lake whitefish are also eaten by big rainbows, the old men of the river.

Finally there are voles, short-tailed mouselike creatures with cream stomachs. Foxes and bears like voles and so do rainbows when the critters fall in.

Alaskan rainbows go for Muddler Minnows from gaudy to plain, sculpin imitations in light to dark colors, weighted and unweighted, also of course dark leech flies, Woolly Buggers, etc. And dry flies, especially those with white wings.

Late one afternoon—eight hours from the lodge and fifteen or more miles up the Alagnak—I noticed that egg flies were hardly working. Could spawning be over up here? As usual some rocky bars were littered with salmon. But these fish, eyeless and leathery, were old. Few freshdeads drifted in the pools.

For days a rigged dry-fly rod of mine lay untouched in the boat. So I got it and handed it to Andy Owens standing beside a shallow pool. *Now for a rest with a cup of tea,* I thought.

I'd turned away when I heard Andy shout, "On the first cast!" He had hooked a rainbow on a white-winged Ausable Wulff, one of those trout that has its own way in the river. Minutes passed before Andy asked for a net to slip under the five-pound fish.

This was a turning point. We quit at seven p.m., worn out. For one thing the graylings came on strong to our drys and, although they were worthwhile, we were after the heart-stoppers; I'm guessing they were about 100 casts apart in this section of river.

The following day was to be my last on the river; all other clients had left, and so had most of the guides. So it was decided that the fishing staff would have a rainbow spree.

As we started upriver with Andy Owens, there were JD Love and his fiancee Sandy, also Bob DeVito. All keen anglers. All excited. All in a desperate hurry. No flies to be tied on for the dudes now. No poor casts to duck and keep silent about. Not a worry in the crowd for it was yet another cloudless day with just an early morning nip to the air. They hit the river running in the knee-deep currents. JD started at a long pool between an island and the shore and instantly was into the rainbows, the run glittering with his leapers. Only a couple of pounds, most of them, but good for the soul.

"What's he using?" I asked DeVito.

"Glow bug," he said, using the local term for an egg fly.

This was a new section of river for me and I prayed that JD Love's early success was an aberration and that black would work.

Soon afterward there was a shout and I glanced upstream. A splendid caribou bull was high-stepping across the current toward an island lush with bushes. Andy dashed to a boat, borrowed a huge revolver from Bob and took off after the

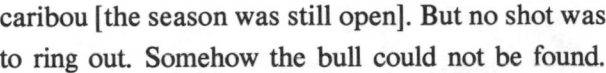

caribou [the season was still open]. But no shot was to ring out. Somehow the bull could not be found.

I saw Sandy struggling with a runner. I saw JD far down the river, fishing hard and fast. Bob was scarcely in sight, working upstream. God knows where Andy was, but happy no doubt.

This was my last chance to fish big and black, and when we moved upriver I picked a stretch for myself. At the same time I wanted last looks at the lovely Alagnak, so clear and inviting, so pristine.

"There are plenty of seven-to-ten pounders," DeVito remarked. "I know because we keep releasing them. But I feel that only now are they returning to their favorite lies after the spawning."

Before evening crowded in on us I'd felt the strength of some good fish, though one of my super Woolly Worms with fluorescent-red body [intended for silver salmon] was better than any all-dark pattern I tried.

There were well-bent rods up and down the river. I hooked three solid fish in three casts and listened to lively reel-talk. And it was enough being on one of the great rainbow rivers of Alaska.

How the others felt after their day's exertions was plain to see. We settled into the boat, not talking much. Every face wore a smile as the good scenes began to play back.

Magic Time

By DENNIS BITTON

HERE'S A TIME on a trout stream—
every day during the summer—when
the sun sets low on the western horizon,
a hatch of some sort comes off, and fish
start to feed. For me, this usually means thirty to
forty-five minutes of "Magic Time" . . . a time when
I can do no wrong.

The fish strike with abandon. I make perfect
presentations. Hookups come every other cast. Fish
brought to hand for release are always beautiful.
And there's never enough time. You do what you
can to make things last: better casts, bringing fish in
quickly, and tying knots faster. [It seems like you
always have to change flies and tipped material
during Magic Time.]

And then it's over. Oh, there are still a few fish

working, and you're still catching them. But it's not like it was. Magic Time is over. It's a special time on the river, and in all her wisdom, Mother Nature makes sure that it's always available . . . in limited amounts. You can *taste* pure happiness, but not for very long.

That doesn't matter. One dose sustains you until the next sunset, the next bit of Magic Time. Sometimes, if you're lucky, you can experience it two or three nights in a row. Sometimes it happens in the middle of the day, and sometimes it happens in the spring or fall. But always, in your memory, it happens at sunset on a summer day.

That's the way you remember it when you're at work, trying to concentrate on making a living. Magic Time interrupts. It comes seeping in under the doorway to your mind. It's a silent, welcome intruder. You sense its presence, and do absolutely nothing to discourage the thoughts, memories and mental images taking shape in your brain. You don't actually *encourage* this mental takeover, but you don't do anything to chase it away either.

Magic Time is for fly fishermen. It may exist for other fishermen, other sportsmen as well. I simply don't know. I'm limited by my background, and I only know about Magic Time on trout streams with a fly rod. From my perspective it's unique, and it deserves some consideration.

Why does it happen? What makes it happen? Why is it so regular? Why does it make you feel good? Why does it stop? How does it stop? What does it all mean?

I've tried to analyze these questions, and have come up with some reasonable answers. But I'm quite certain reason has little to do with it.

I guess some biologist could give me a good explanation for Magic Time. But I don't want one. I like the feeling of moving at 33 rpm and then the surging sensation as everything in and around the river seems to speed up to 45 rpm.

"It's Magic Time!"

I say that, out loud, every time it happens. Fishing partners give me a weird look, but I know what's coming. It's going to happen this time just like it did the last time, and it's going to be fantastic. With this kind of high, you need no artificial stimulants.

Magic Time is for little boys who need it. Magic Time is for old men and working, middle-aged men who need it too. Magic Time is not for certain people. It falls on everyone, just like rain. But then, like rain, you have to appreciate it. If rain just means a cold shower to you, then you probably won't appreciate that a little rain makes the plants grow greener. And if you're that insensitive, I doubt that you've ever experienced Magic Time anyway.

Too bad. That's what it's all about. "Magic Time!"

BIOLOGICAL TIPPETS

Peter Barrett was outdoors editor for *True Magazine* from 1947 to 1954. In 1955 he held a similar post at *Sports Illustrated.* Peter landed his first article at *Field & Stream* in 1961, and is fishing editor of that magazine. His outdoor adventures include 12 African safaris.

Dennis Bitton, editor of *The Flyfisher,* magazine of The Federation of Fly Fishers, has been a consistent voice in promoting good will for the sport. Dennis also wears the cap of editor of *Flyfishing News,* a tabloid. Both publications are based in Big Sky country.

Silvio Calabi is the editor of *Rod & Reel,* subtitled *The Journal of American Flyfishing.* He's also wader-deep into another publication, *Fly-Tackle Dealer.* Both are published by the Camden, Maine-based outfit, Down East Enterprises. Silvio writes a lean sentence, casts a mean fly.

Jay H. Cassell has been Senior Editor of *Sports Afield* since 1979. Earlier in his career he was an editor at *Outdoor Life.* His articles have appeared in *Business Week, Vista, New Jersey Monthly,* among others. A "master" in the stream, he holds a Masters in Journalism from Syracuse.

Ed Gray is the publisher-editor of one of America's most treasured [and collected] outdoors publications, *Gray's Sporting Journal,* published in Massachusetts. As his tale in this volume attests, he is also a first-rate storyteller and appreciator of the folklore of fishing.

Nick Lyons is the founder of Lyons & Burford, which specializes in fly fishing titles. When he was executive editor at Crown Publishers, he created the

-more-

highly regarded Sportsman Classic series. Nick taught English literature at Hunter College for 25 years.

John Randolph is editor-publisher at *Fly Fisherman,* out of Cowles Magazines in Harrisburg, PA. Earlier he was managing editor of *Backpacker,* and editor-in-chief of *Country Journal.* His writing has appeared in *Field & Stream, Outdoor Life, Sports Afield, Vermont Life.*

Marty Sherman sold his first article to *Fly Fishing the West* in 1978, and in 1984 he became editor of *Fly Fishing Magazine,* published by Amato in Portland, OR. Marty began to fly fish at age nine in Alaska. In 1965 he moved to Oregon so he could fish for steelheads all year.

Gary Soucie is executive editor at *Audubon,* a professor of environmental reporting at NYU, and has been a mover-and-shaker at Friends of the Earth and the Sierra Club. His fishing books have been published by Holt Rinehart, and Lyons, with two forthcoming from Fireside.

Vin T. Sparano has been an outdoor editor and writer for nearly three decades. After an early spin at *Sports Afield,* he joined *Outdoor Life,* where he is now the executive editor. Vin is the author-editor of five books, including *The Complete Outdoors Encyclopedia.*

Lamar Underwood, at 33, became the youngest editor of a national magazine when he took over at *Sports Afield* in 1970. Six years later he became editor of *Outdoor Life* and remained there for three years. Lamar is editorial director of the Outdoor Group at Harris Publ. in NYC.